CUSTOMIZE
YOUR CLOTHES

Books published by Running Press are available at special
discounts for bulk purchases in the United States by
corporations, institutions, and other organizations. For more
information, please contact the Special Markets Department
at the Perseus Books Group, 2300 Chestnut Street, Suite 200,
Philadelphia, PA 19103, or call (800) 810-4145, ext. 5000,
or e-mail special.markets@perseusbooks.com.

ISBN 978-0-7624-4347-5
Library of Congress Control Number: 2011936935

9 8 7 6 5 4 3 2 1
Digit on the right indicates the number of this printing

Cover design by Emily Portnoi
Interior design concept by Charlotte Heal
Layout by Victoria Avery
Art directed by Emily Portnoi
Commissioning Editor: Isheeta Mustafi
Edited by Lorraine Slipper
Photography by Dorn Byg
Typography: Flama and Bell

Running Press Book Publishers
2300 Chestnut Street
Philadelphia, PA 19103-4371

Visit us on the web!
www.runningpress.com

CUSTOMIZE
YOUR CLOTHES

A Head-to-Toe Guide to Reinventing Your Wardrobe

RAIN BLANKEN

RUNNING PRESS
PHILADELPHIA · LONDON

CONTENTS

INTRODUCTION

Clothing customization has come a long way since the explosion of puffy paint onto the sweatshirt scene in the late 1980s. Hand embellishments and chic fashion have since come full circle, having perhaps collided somewhere in a parallel universe where Rosy the Riveter lunches with Lady Gaga. Suddenly it's hip to craft our own clothing, and our wardrobes will never be the same again.

In truth, we've simply started sharing our otherwise late-night craft binges with like-minded fashionistas thousands of miles away—and at lightning-fast speed. Social networking sites have encouraged up-to-the-second updates on projects, feedback, and tutorials. Broadcasts are sent to our homes, offices, and even our pockets, effectively sky-rocketing the exposure of handmade design. The craft activity of the world is now on tap to fuel the creative spirit that was once confined to local sewing circles and the occasional craft show.

The chapters ahead include design photos that traverse the spectrum of the fashion world. From haphazard bleach spatters to painstakingly stitched embroidery—a treasure trove of color, fabric, and inventive design has been provided for you to refresh your creative spirit each time you open this book.

Top: Beaded cardigan. See page 98.
Bottom: Block-printed skirt. See page 58.

While working the tutorials, remember that the gallery designs are prime examples of each technique. Respect the original ideas of these independent artists by avoiding duplication of their work. Instead, compliment them by making your own creations inspired by the talent that came before you.

The following step-by-step tutorials have been constructed with alterations in mind. I invite you to use these techniques as a springboard. Get familiar with the methods involved, browse the kaleidoscope of designs in the galleries and interviews, and then apply these new ideas to your wardrobe. Somewhere along the way, your crafty side will make friends with your stylish side.

Above: Spray-painted shoes.
See page 41.

Right: Dip-dyed arm warmers.
See page 38.

Chapter 1

WHY CUSTOMIZE?

"Always be a first-rate version of yourself, instead of a second-rate version of somebody else"

— Judy Garland

Well, who doesn't? Even the act of staring into your closet and cobbling together your daily outfit is a form of customizing your look. We've all gotten by with unexpected trips to the grocery store in sweat pants and an old t-shirt, but even these hurried outfits have a premeditated flavor to them. My t-shirt bears Hello Kitty's adorable mug and I decided on these sneakers six months ago. Without even trying, we're all silently screaming our personalities in the produce aisle.

This effortless transmission will become what people drum up in their memories of you. Your clothes are an expression as memorable as the look on your face. It is only natural that we try to control our look as much as we can. If you can change your whole look with a single article of clothing, then imagine what can be achieved when you customize each piece.

When you are in control of every piece of clothing you own, then suddenly your fashion possibilities have grown a thousand fold. A zipper here, some paint

there, and your look has changed dramatically. Not only that, but you have just recycled a piece of clothing that might have otherwise ended up in a landfill.

Clothing customization can also save you some money. No need to spend your savings at a high-end boutique when you can achieve your own couture at home. Name-brand fashion often applies many of the simple techniques found in this book. The next time you are at the mall, see how many factory-made fashions you could make at home. So far you are saving money, feeding the creative spirit, and even doing your part to recycle. Not bad for a day's work. Therein lies the self-confidence that our handicraft provides. Custom clothes are sustainable, affordable, and made to look just as you pictured them. They are unlike anything else in the world, and styled exactly to suit you. That is the difference between your clothes and Your Clothes.

The Search for Individuality

Clothes are our public skin—nothing short of our armor and costume. In 1966 John Lennon wore a gold-braided military band jacket to a *Life* magazine photo shoot. That coat sold for $240,000 at a Beverly Hills auction in 2010. Lennon made the conscious decision to wear this particular coat that day, choosing it specifically to express himself in photographs where his rapier wit might be absent. Today we still identify the Lennon legacy with imagery of Sgt. Pepper jackets and tinted circle lenses.

You might not be John Lennon (or the current owner of a $240,000 jacket for that matter), but style sticks with all of us in the same way. Fashion is perhaps the most personal of the visual arts. It is the art that we associate ourselves with so closely that it is literally rubbing right up against our skin. Love a painting, and it remains on the wall. Wear a dress, and it is synonymous with your name as soon as you walk into the room.

Self-expression comes in many forms, from doodling while you're on the phone to posting your "Likes" on Facebook. Even if you wouldn't describe yourself as having a style that fits into one specific genre, there is most likely a set of parameters that define your signature "look." With this in mind, how do you feel about the clothes in your closet right now? What would you do to make them more … you?

Left: Handpainted high heels by Shadow Empress Studios.

It is common these days to cross our fingers and hope that someone else isn't wearing the same dress on a big night out. Why are we taking such a back seat to our individuality? All of us want to look like something different, or else we'd all be walking around in silver jumpsuits by now (thank goodness 1950s sci-fi was wrong). When you decide to add ribbon trim to that party dress, this isn't just a crafty practice, it's also a proactive way to claim your signature look. Not only that, but now you've got something to say about your crafty prowess while fielding compliments.

What you want out of fashion can be hard to achieve when you are only given the limited pool of options presented to you at the mall. Branch out to find what you love, then add your own flavor to it until you've got something truly unique. Years from now someone might reflect on your look. What will they say?

Above: Tie-dyed pants. See page 44.
Right: Hand-colored dress. See page 76.

Sustainable Fashion

Fashion, while very personal, is also the most fickle of arts. What we wear today could make us cringe when we flip through the photo album in a few years. With this kind of impermanence and often glaring hindsight, what's here today is often gone tomorrow. This is an age of environmentally conscious society, and the disposable fashion world is falling behind the chic green trend.

It can be fun to keep a pulse on the seasonal fashion trends, but these should be seen as a set of guidelines drawn up by the fashion industry, not a death sentence to last season's sweater. While our clothing acts as the costume we step out of the house in, it is much closer to the heart than fashion gurus would have us think. This is the reason our closets are often filled to bursting before we finally break down and decide what to keep and what to give away. Years can pass without wearing a garment, yet the attachment remains.

The next time you are faced with a bounty of forgotten clothes, consider adjusting these pieces to fit your style instead of turning them over to the fashion police. Whether out of season, stained, or torn, clothes can live many lives before they are finally reduced to rags. Dye, for instance, can turn an autumn shirt into a bright spring blouse … and maybe even conceal a stain in the process. Holes in jeans can be rocked as-is or covered with a cute patch. Accidentally bleached something? Spritz it all over in bleach and suddenly you've got a happy accident instead of a ruined bag.

A trip to the thrift store can yield valuable finds if you know how to make your clothes do your bidding. Suddenly you aren't surrounded by yesteryear's fashion, but rather a room full of blank canvases. You will soon be able to pick out the scarf that could use your embroidery know-how, and which bag would look great with a block print on the flap. Make it a challenge. Don't dismiss any sweater because it is so last season … figure out a way to wear it again because it deserves another run.

Right: Junky Styling deconstruct, re-cut, and transform second-hand clothing into "high-fashion street couture."

Upcycling

Did you know that there is a purse in your jeans, or that your sweater has a secret desire to be a skirt? Upcycling involves the use of common materials and conventional methods to transform everyday or damaged clothing into high-quality versions of themselves … or a purse.

Upcycling is like a glamorous magic trick for your clothes. Step right up and witness two t-shirts turn into a hoodie right before your very eyes. Witness a man's shirt evolve into a chic evening dress. Poof! The before and after photos alone are enough to make you smile.

The term "upcycled" was coined by William McDonough and Michael Braungart in their 2002 book *Cradle to Cradle: Remaking the Way We Make Things*. An architect and a chemist respectively, these men were describing the process of converting an otherwise useless material into something of similar or greater value. I can't think of a better term for an extra-large New Kids on the Block t-shirt than "useless material." The same shirt as a scarf? Now that is just funny enough to work.

While impressive, upcycling doesn't have to be that complicated. If you are adding quality and function to something that would have otherwise rotted in a landfill (or your basement) then you are upcycling. Improve upon a flimsy store-bought bag with bead embellishments and a patch of your own design. Even creating fingerless gloves by cutting off holey glove fingers is upcycling.

Enjoy the meditative qualities that crafting can afford while shrinking your carbon footprint. This resourceful approach to breathing new life into unwanted clothing puts you right at the forefront of "green fashion" while feeding the creative soul. What could you make a t-shirt into? How would you turn a sweatshirt into a tote?

Top: This tote bag from People Tree is made from recycled sari fabrics.

Bottom: Jana Foehrenbach of Broken Ghost Couture upcycles second-hand and vintage clothes to create unique clothing.

Vintage patterns can be a valuable source of inspiration.

Research

The best way to learn about fashion is to just keep looking at it. Absorb monthly runway magazines one page at a time. Teach yourself to recognize what you like about each design, how it makes you feel, and whether or not you would wear it.

Take a stroll through clothing stores and make a note of what you would buy—with the theoretical stipulation that you could only buy one thing. What would you walk out with? Check out not only what the mannequins are wearing, but also the other shoppers.

Look at vintage designs. The origin of certain pieces, pencil skirts for instance, can give you insight into how styles evolve over the years. Ask yourself what happened to Victorian bloomers and hippie bell-bottoms. Did they disappear overnight or slowly morph into other fashions? Versions of these far-out fashions may work well when incorporated into your own designs.

Flip to the back of this book for a lot of websites that will help you research the looks and techniques you love. Included are the shops of the independent designers featured in this book, who have come up with ideas that are light years ahead of the big box stores. These artists most likely started out just like us, curiously flipping through the pages of a craft book and telling themselves, "This just might be for me." And, like you, they probably even started to dream up which project to try first before even leaving the bookstore.

Go home and fail a few times. Try to sew a pattern of tiny beads onto a stretchy shirt. Spray a wool sweater with bleach and watch it disintegrate. Wear a color you've suspected will look terrible on you. Whether you mess up or not, hands-on experiments are a valuable part of the research. Through trial and error you will not only find some answers, but you'll also come up with a lot of questions you didn't know you had.

Sketching Designs

Getting your ideas on paper is an important process that often reaps surprising results. You might start with a hat design, only to come up with the perfect bead embellishment for a pair of gloves. On the other hand, sketching can bring intense focus to a design, leading you to pin down all the details of a screen print in a matter of minutes.

Sketching helps us to compare how colors and textures will work together in a design. Color and texture are dynamic. That is, our eyes are constantly reading these elements according to what is directly next to them. A better scientist than I would tell you that this is an interaction between the light receptors in our eyes and the light spectrum that surrounds us.

For the rest of us, this means that a dark cotton shirt can look bland paired with jeans—but switch it up with tweed slacks and the softness of the shirt is instantly showcased. These simple fashion tricks also apply to the micro-managed color and texture pairing in clothing customization. Be sure to include color and texture in your sketched designs.

Many times we find the look we want before deciding which piece of clothing to customize. For example, if you like the look of fabric flowers, you might have them visualized before you've even perused the closet for a shirt to experiment on. Draw out these pieces while they are still fresh in your mind, even if you don't plan to work on them for a while.

When planning a piece of clothing that you would like to customize, try loosely sketching it many times on the same page. Truly brainstorm on these, trying out every design that comes to you, no matter how tame or wacky. Sometimes the craziest of ideas will produce a classic design.

Sketches by Kate Gallagher

WHY CUSTOMIZE?

TUTORIAL

Generating Artworks: Photoshop

With all the technology available today, it's never been easier to create your own works of art. All you need is a computer and a program like Photoshop—sketching skills are not required! Just use a photo to make a truly unique and individual addition to your clothes.

16

Friends and family make great subjects for this project because artistic prints of them are probably hard to find in a department store. I chose my furry friend, Riley, to help us with this tutorial because, well, her face is just so entertaining.

The following instructions are given for version 7 of Adobe Photoshop. If you are using a different version or a different picture-editing program, please refer to your manual or online help documents for instructions.

Before You Begin

Choose a high-resolution photo (at least 300dpi) of a subject that is simple and in focus. In Photoshop, click the Windows drop-down menu at the top of the screen to make sure that the Tools and Layers options are selected. Open your photo in Photoshop. Visit the View drop-down menu to display the image as Print Size so that it is easy to work with.

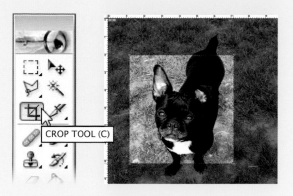

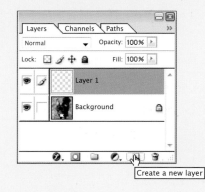

1 | Crop to Focus on Your Subject
Use the Crop tool in the Tool Box to crop the photo closer to the subject that you would like to turn into a print.

I am going for Riley's head, so I pulled it in close, but left a little room to work in.

2 | Create a Blank Layer
(A) Select the Create New Layer button in the Layers palette. This will make a blank layer appear on top of your photo.

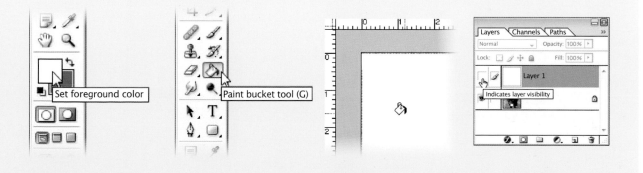

(B) In the Tool Box, select Set Foreground Color. Select white, and then click Okay.

(C) Click the Paint Bucket Tool.

(D) Be sure that your new layer is still selected in the Layers palette, then click anywhere on your canvas. The entire layer will turn white, but don't worry—our doggie is still in there!

(E) In the Layers palette, click the eyeball next to your new white layer. This hides it from view until we need to use it later.

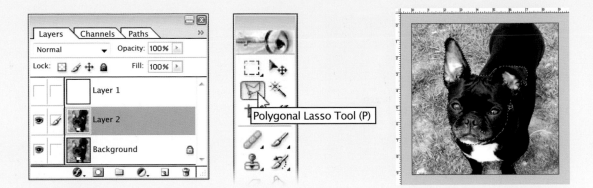

3 Eliminate the Background

(A) The Background layer is locked, so we need to make a copy of it to work with. Click on the Background layer in the Layers palette. Select the entire photo by pressing Ctrl+A (Cmd-A on Mac) and copy it to the clipboard by pressing Ctrl+C (Cmd-C on Mac). Paste the copied image right over the background layer by pressing Ctrl+V (Cmd-V on Mac). This should show up as Layer 2 in your Layers palette.

(B) Click and drag Layer 2 so that it is above our white Layer 1. Unhide Layer 1. You still won't be able to see it because Layer 2 is now in the way.

(C) In the Tool Box, select the Polygonal Lasso tool. Click around the part of the subject that you would like to use as a print. Play with the Zoom feature in the View menu if you need a closer look. Create a complete shape by ending your selection where you began. A tiny circle will appear next to your lasso cursor when you have made your way back to the beginning.

(D) Once you have finished your selection, go to the Select menu and click Inverse. This will select the background instead of your subject.

Press Delete. The background will disappear, leaving only what you want to print in front of the white background.

4 Make it Printable

Now you can print the image onto heat transfer paper for iron-ons. You can also put it on just about anything by pasting another photo into this file. Today though, we want to create an image that will work well with stamping and screen printing, so we are going to turn the image into a flat silhouette.

Go to the Image menu and click the Adjustments submenu. From here, click Threshold. With this tool, you can adjust how your high-contrast image will look. Make sure that the Preview box is checked while you play with this tool. Click Okay and you've got a high-contrast image ready to send to the printer.

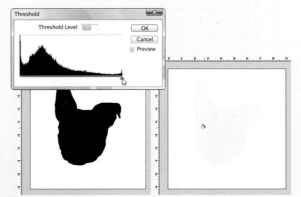

5 One Step Further: Multicolored Prints

(A) In addition to a one-color image, this technique can also be used to get a few different degrees of contrast, which can then be layered in the printing process to make a multicolored print. To do this, go back to Step 3 and select your Layer 2 image after the background has been eliminated. Copy and Paste the image as many times as you need for your different levels of contrast. Hide all of these layers except for Layer 2 and the white background layer (Layer 1).

(B) On Layer 2 adjust the Threshold so that the image is as completely solid as you can make it. Select a bright foreground color and use the Paint Bucket Tool to fill the shape. I chose yellow. Make sure the Contiguous option at the top of the screen is unchecked as you work with the Paint Bucket tool.

(C) Unhide Layer 3. Adjust the Threshold on Layer 3 to around the middle of the bar. You've got more detail now, but things are still looking pretty black. Click the Magic Wand tool in the Tool Box. Make sure Contiguous is not checked in the options at the top of the screen. Click on any white area inside your image. This will select all of the white areas on this layer. Press the Delete button. Now you can see through to the bright layer below. Go to the Select menu and click Deselect. Use the Paint Bucket tool to again fill in your solid areas on this layer with a bright color.

(D) Repeat with each following layer, using the Threshold tool to adjust the silhouettes so that the print area decreases each time. When it is time to print your images, hide all of the layers except the one you want to print. On the Print Preview screen, select Registration Marks to help you align your layers on a series of woodblocks or screens for printing. Now you can print your photo in different stages of contrast, allowing for a multicolored print.

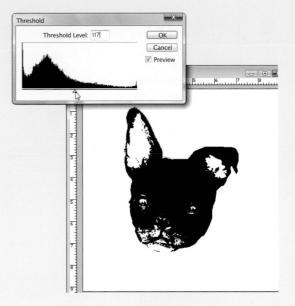

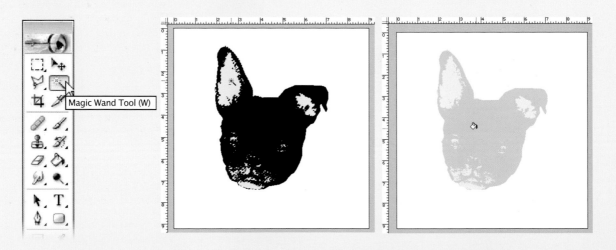

Magic Wand Tool (W)

Placing Graphics

The chest of a t-shirt seems to be prime real estate for design placement, but I would like to invite you to consider the alternatives to the "billboard" look when you apply print designs to clothing. Here are a few ideas for graphic placement that you may want to consider.

T-Shirt Prints

- **The Scatter Effect**
  Print a repeating pattern all over the shirt, but give it personality, for example, make it look as though it were being blown in by the wind on one side, or falling from on top.

- **Full Coverage**
  Print a shirt with a large design so that it wraps around the side, onto the sleeves, and even meanders around the back. Animals, words, and scenery are great for this kind of print.

- **Imperfect Prints**
  When you print, there are times when the color doesn't transfer to the material just right. It could be a wrinkle in the fabric or just a case of too much ink. Try to roll with it. Sometimes a printing "whoops" can become the best thing you've ever done. If it looks great, just nod, smile, and take full credit.

Other Hot Spots to Try

- **Sleeves**
  A single shirt sleeve can be printed in lots of ways. Patterned designs look good carefully applied down the arm from the shoulder to the wrist. Another option is to work at an angle from the shoulder to the cuff, or even from the cuff to the neck. For short sleeves, try printing all around the sleeve hem.

- **Pant Cuffs**
  Create small prints along the bottom of your pants that look as if they might be trying to find their way up the outer seam.

- **Scarves**
  Keep in mind that when you are printing on scarves, the two ends will be the most visible when they are worn. Scarves work well with small, repeated patterns and motifs. If you are going for a larger design, print on the ends.

- **Purses**
  Fabric purses and totes have a nice flat surface for adding a design. Go for the flaps on messenger bags, and consider using the same print on a matching coin purse.

- **Hoods**
  Off the top of my head, hoods are a great place to print animal ears, horns, or even block lettering. This is an often overlooked area.

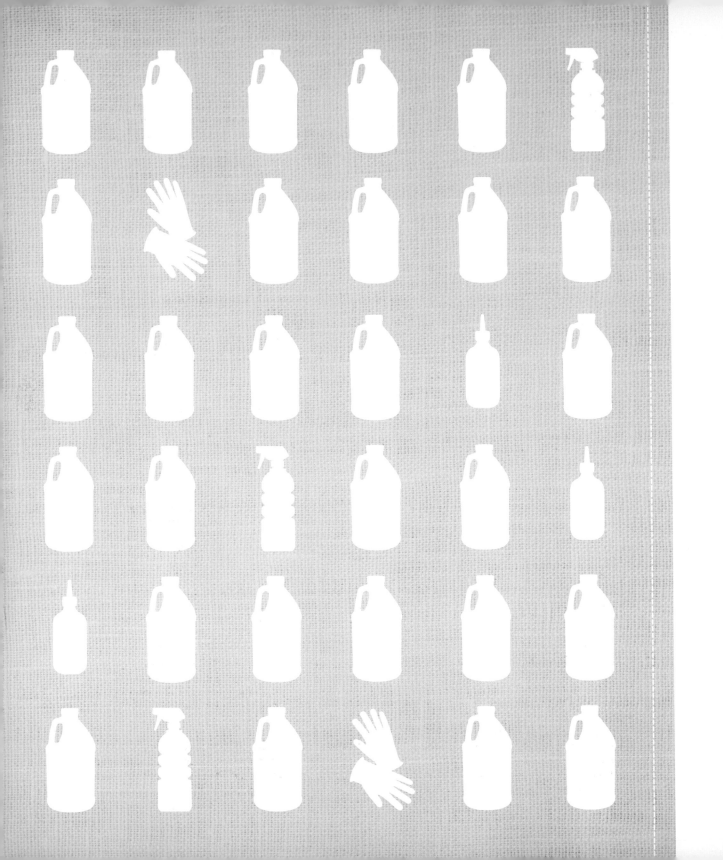

Chapter 2

BLEACHING

"Is negative space the space you don't like, or the space that is not there? And if it's not there, how can you tell?"

— Emma Bull, *Finder*

Outside of the laundry room, bleached clothing is nothing short of chemically-enhanced style. When you add a bleaching agent to clothes, you are actually inducing a molecular reaction that removes the color, or "discharges" the previously set dye from the material. In this chapter, we will show you how to remove color from your clothing to create negative space and bright line art.

A course in bleaching calls for geeking out on some fashion science. Fabrics vary in their chemical composition and will react differently to discharging. Plant-derived (cellulose) fibers work best with bleach. These include the denim in your jeans, canvas bags, and other common clothing materials like cotton, rayon, and linen. Man-made (synthetic) materials are not recommended, as they are very resistant to discharging. These include nylon, acrylic, and polyester. Synthetic/cellulose blends like poly-cotton will yield modest results.

Do not use chlorine bleach on animal-derived (protein) fibers such as silk, wool, and angora—they will instantly scorch. For these, try a discharge paste instead. Thicker than liquid bleach and much less corrosive, discharge paste can be used for controlled color removal by stamp, stencil, or brush techniques. Discharge paste may seem obscure, but it is inexpensive and readily available online and in craft stores.

Always test an unnoticeable patch of the garment first to see how it will react before going whole-hog with color removal. Fabrics will not always turn completely white, but the longer you leave the discharge agent on, the paler your color will be.

Chlorine bleach is corrosive, which means that it will not only break down the color in the fabric, but also eat away at the fibers until they disintegrate. It is important to work with a "stop agent" that will terminate the action of the bleach. Your stop bath should always be ready before you start bleaching. In this chapter, we will be using 3% hydrogen peroxide, which is available at your local drugstore.

Even the most stylish of mad scientists knows that safety comes first. Only work with discharge agents in a well-ventilated area, and always wear rubber gloves. Never mix bleach with discharge paste or other ammonia-based products. Read the updated safety information on your chemical label so that you are well prepared in case of spills, and for Pete's sake, don't eat it!

Now it's time to marry this fashion science with art. Let's explore a few methods of bleaching that go beyond simply dumping Clorox on your whites.

BLEACHING

TUTORIAL

Abstracts

Spatters on clothing can transform a drab shirt into a spontaneous pattern or assist in fading jeans. A spray bottle is a good way to safely apply droplets of bleach without a lot of accidents.

24

What You'll Need:

- **A dark-colored garment**
- **Cardboard**
- **Scissors**
- **Spray-mount adhesive**
- **Spray bottle**
- **Rubber gloves**
- **Paper towels**
- **Bleach**
- **Water**
- **Sink or tub to rinse**
- **Hydrogen peroxide**

Get Prepared:

To perfect our skills at abstract bleaching, we will mist a chlorine bleach mixture onto a garment to create a variety of solid and speckled areas. I added an octopus silhouette to this shirt to make use of the appearance of bubbles and add a theme to the piece, but this technique would also work great with a space theme, with the addition of rocket and meteor cutouts.

Bleach will ruin some surfaces and fabrics, so wear clothing that you don't mind sacrificing, and cover your work area with a piece of plastic or cardboard. Wear gloves whenever handling the bleach and work in a well-ventilated area. Immediately wipe up any bleach spills.

Before you get started, prepare your hydrogen peroxide bath so that you can stop the bleach from over-developing later. Mix eight parts water to one part hydrogen peroxide in a tub large enough to submerge the garment.

1 | **Cut the Stencil and Insert Cardboard**
Freehand a simple design, or trace a stencil onto cardboard, and cut it out. You will need cardboard in the garment to prevent the bleach from bleeding through to the other side and to prevent wrinkling under the silhouette. To create the wrap around design of this shirt, I made sure that the right-side seam was also on top of the cardboard. I put a small insert into the right-hand sleeve, too.

2 | **Spray Adhesive onto the Silhouette**
Lightly apply a thin coat of spray adhesive onto the back of the stencil. This is important, as the liquid bleach can seep under the edges of the stencil if it is not secured. Use a minimal amount of adhesive and let it dry to a tacky film before applying.

3 | **Apply the Silhouette to the Garment**
Think about where you want to spray the bleach before you apply the stencil. Mounting adhesive is gentle when applied properly, so you should be able to reposition the stencil several times.

4 | **Prepare and Spray the Bleach**
Mix one part bleach with one part water in your spray bottle. Pure bleach would be too harsh on the fabric. Use a spare piece of cardboard to test your misting technique before you spray the garment. A fine mist over the stencil worked well to create a solid background behind it. I sprayed in an "L" shape down the right side and bottom of the shirt to create the bubbly extensions.

BLEACHING | Abstracts

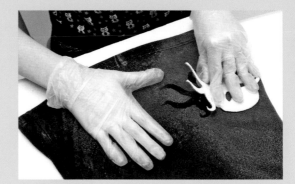

5 **Add Details**
A spritz will create individual bubbles, while a fine mist will join to fade the entire sleeve. I created individual droplets on the right-hand sleeve of my shirt. I also dotted the cuff of the left-hand sleeve with a few bubbles to match.

6 **Develop the Garment and Remove the Silhouette**
Even before you are done spraying, you may notice the garment changing color. Simply watch the garment to determine when you want to stop the bleach from developing the color. Wait no more than 10 minutes to prevent damage to the fabric. Carefully peel up the stencil. Adhesive residue can be picked off by hand.

7 **Rinse and Stop**
Rinse your garment under running water for a full minute, and then put it in the hydrogen peroxide bath. Leave it to soak for five to 10 minutes. Rinse it one more time, then hang it up to dry.

Motifs and Artworks

TUTORIAL

Stenciling and splattering bleach can produce great graphic results, but there is a way to remove color with increased precision and artistic freedom. Modern science has recently brought about the miracle of the bleach pen, a dispenser used to spot-treat stained garments. However, I prefer to use it on undamaged garments to turn them into absolutely fantastic works of art.

What You'll Need:

- Chalk
- Rubber gloves
- Paper towels
- Bleach pen
- Sink or tub
- Water
- Hydrogen peroxide

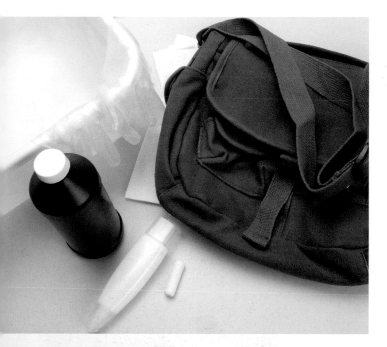

Get Prepared:

Bleach pens are ideal for creating more intricate designs and for adding words to a piece. For this project, I chose to add lyrics from The White Stripes' "Rag and Bone" to a canvas bag. This bag was made for my personal use only; if you decide to use song lyrics or any other copyrighted text for your projects, do not attempt to sell your work as the words remain the property of the band or writer.

Bleach will ruin some surfaces and fabrics. Wear clothing that you don't mind sacrificing, and cover your work area with a piece of plastic or cardboard. Wear your gloves whenever handling the bleach and work in a well-ventilated area. Immediately wipe up any bleach accidents.

Before you get started, prepare your hydrogen peroxide bath so that you can stop the bleach from over-developing later. Mix eight parts water to one part hydrogen peroxide in a tub large enough to submerge the piece.

BLEACHING | Motifs and Artworks

1 | Chalk it Out

Draw your design in chalk before you bleach. Chalk can easily be wiped off in case of mistakes, and will not chemically react with the bleach. Get creative with your pictures, or stick with simple shapes like stars and hearts if you aren't much of an artist. Don't get too intricate, or it will be a pain to trace.

2 | Write it in Bleach

Put on the rubber gloves and carefully trace over your chalk lines. If your bleach pen bubbles at the end, dab it on paper towels to pop the bubble and return to a nice bleach flow. Retain tension on the pen as you trace to keep the application smooth. The bleach will develop very quickly as you draw.

3 | Spray Adhesive onto the Silhouette

Rinse the piece under running water, using your gloved hand to quickly knock off the bleach. Dip it into the hydrogen peroxide bath as soon as you have cleared away the bleach chunks. Soak for five to 10 minutes, then rinse again for a full minute.

4 | Repeat on the Back

To create a design on the back of your piece, you will need to wait until it has been fully rinsed and dried. Work on the back as you did the front. Try longer developing times for different areas of your design. Here, the bleach paste on the lyrics and "rag and bone" wagon were allowed to cure for longer, resulting in a bright orange. Meanwhile, the horse was only allowed a few seconds to develop, and was stopped at a deep red. Plan your design carefully so that you can utilize the gradually changing colors of the bleached fabric.

Lyrics from the song "Rag and Bone" by The White Stripes Written by Jack White.

BLEACHING

TUTORIAL Basic Patterns

Liquid bleach can be hard to work with because it is so caustic and runny. Discharge paste is a good alternative, because it can be used on sensitive fabrics like silk and will hold its shape to create precise patterns. Use it with fabrics that can safely be steam ironed—discharge paste is activated by heat.

What You'll Need:

- Thin garment, such as a scarf
- Cardboard
- Scissors
- Spray-mount adhesive
- Sponge brush
- Discharge paste
- Iron
- Ironing board
- Sink or tub
- Water

Get Prepared:

Scarves are a great candidate for discharge paste because they are thin and often made of delicate materials that can't be bleached.

Discharge paste can ruin some surfaces and fabrics, so, as with bleach, wear clothing that you don't mind sacrificing, and cover your work area with a piece of plastic or cardboard. Wear gloves whenever handling the discharge paste and work in a well-ventilated area.

1 | **Choose the Stencil**
I decided to create my own stencils for this scarf, but you can use a commercially bought stencil, too. You can even print a design from your computer and trace it onto cardboard.

2 | **Prepare the Stencil**
Lightly apply the spray-mount adhesive to the stencil. You will be removing and repositioning the stencil many times, so a light coating is imperative. Use a minimal amount of adhesive and let it dry to a tacky film before applying.

3 | **Position the Stencil**
Lay your piece on a sheet of cardboard or another smooth, protective surface. Place the stencil and press firmly, making sure that the fabric is not wrinkled underneath.

4 | **Apply the Discharge Paste**
Use your sponge brush to dab the discharge paste onto the stencil. Try not to push the paste through to the other side of the fabric because it could get squashed under the stencil and create blobs of removed color. If you make a mistake, apply a dab of hydrogen peroxide to the area that you would like to prevent from getting developed.

32

5 | **Remove the Stencil and Wait**
Wait 10 minutes to an hour for the paste to dry. The more paste you apply, the longer it will take to dry. Use this time to carefully lift your stencil and apply a pattern of designs to your piece. You can move on to the next step while it is still wet if you are happy with a slightly distorted look. For fine lines, be patient and wait out the dry time.

6 | **Iron the Discharge Paste**
Use a dish towel under your work while ironing to prevent the paste from distorting the color of your ironing-board cover. Set the iron on the lowest steam setting and press the stenciled area for at least 10 seconds. If your discharge paste is still wet, avoid sliding the iron from side-to-side. As the discharge paste activates, it will begin to stink up the place with an ammonia gas, so always iron in a well-ventilated area.

7 | **Witness the Magic of Discharge Paste**
When you lift your iron, you will be greeted with the results of your labor. Depending on how well you filled in the stencil and whether or not the discharge paste was dry, you should get a high-contrast design that can transform an old garment into a new favorite.

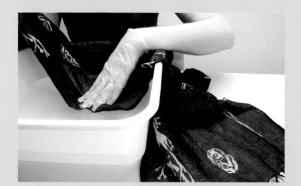

8 | **Rinse**
Discharge paste can hold an ammonia stink on your clothing until it is washed. Rinse the garment in water and wash with detergent to remove the discharge paste residue.

Raygun Robyn

Raygun Robyn is a one-woman army, bringing the world unique t-shirts and bags, armed only with a spray bottle. Her designs combine futuristic monsters and retro robots and aim to make you look awesome. Raygun Robyn hails from Mars and is here to conquer Earth.

www.raygunrobyn.com

Robot SMASH bag.

34

How did you get interested in using bleach as a medium?

I had been making appliqué shirts for a while when I ran across a tutorial using bleach and was instantly hooked. I love how each shirt I make is different, even if it is the same design. I also love how I can get an idea for a design, mock up a stencil, and see my idea come to fruition all in the same day.

Where do you find inspiration for your designs?

I like to make things that I would personally wear and I'm a nerd and sci-fi geek at heart, so a lot of my designs feature monsters, robots, and spaceships. Not cutesy monsters, but real, "OH NO, RUN" kind of stuff. I watched a ton of old sci-fi movies and TV shows in my youth so I think it's just ingrained in my neurons.

What is the most challenging aspect of bleach art?

One of the most challenging things about using bleach is trying to get clean lines and detail. Bleach is also a corrosive material, so I have to be sure to clean all my materials so they don't fall apart. I've had a couple of stencils break on me and it's the saddest thing. Bleach eats through super glue like nobody's business!

What was the catalyst that turned your craft into "Raygun Robyn" the business?

I've always had some side business that I would use for my creative outlet. I got frustrated with the assorted and weird day jobs, so I decided I'd had my fill of working for other people and really focused on getting Raygun Robyn on its feet. It's been a long process and a learning experience. My recent success has been based on building a group of fans, making great products, and making people happy.

How important do you think online selling sites are to independent artists?

Selling online is key for independent artists, and learning how to market yourself and find new avenues and niches to explore. I can live anywhere in the world and still successfully run Raygun Robyn.

BLEACHING | Gallery

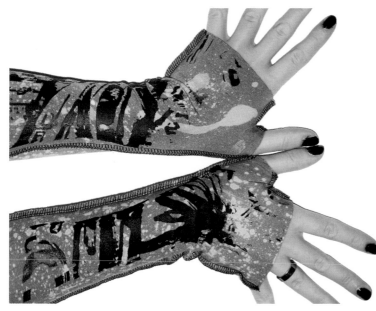

Bleached and screen-printed gloves by PopLove Designs.

Bleached t-shirt by ContreLeJour.

Bleached silk scarf by Jane Porter.

Bleached canvas tote bag by ContreLeJour.

Chapter 3 |

COLORING

"Life is short, use all the colors in the crayon box"

— RuPaul

With paints and dyes, old shirts are instantly renewed and stained pants can keep a secret. But dyeing and painting involve a lot of chemical reactions. Fabrics have different molecular structures, so you have to have the right material for the job. Some dyes are dangerous to inhale, while others remain relatively tame. It is important to know what you are getting into before mixing up a big ol' vat of chartreuse.

In the last chapter we briefly discussed cellulose (plant), synthetic (man-made), and protein (animal) fibers, each of which has a different reaction to bleach. They also have different ideas about accepting color.

Fiber-reactive dyes work well with cellulose fibers like cotton, rayon, and hemp. The molecules in fiber-reactive dye actually fuse with the fiber molecules, creating a permanent bond. This is the kind of dye usually found in tie-dye kits because t-shirts are generally made from cotton or a mostly cotton blend.

Acid dyes are used on protein fibers like mohair, feathers, or wool. While the term "acid dye" may sound a bit scary, this involves a mild acid such as white vinegar. The acid works to lower the pH of the fiber so it will readily accept the dye.

All-purpose dyes are easily found in grocery stores, and will do for blends between cellulose and protein fabrics. However, they can only be used with hot water, and produce less vibrant results than fiber-reactive or acid dyes alone.

There are a couple of rogue materials that can be dyed despite their categorization. Silk, a protein fiber, can take fiber-reactive dyes as well as cotton. Nylon, a synthetic fiber, responds well to an acid-dye process and all-purpose dyes. Other synthetic fibers require specialized chemicals and hard-to-find dyes. Some synthetics cannot be dyed at all, such as polyester/spandex blends. If you have a polyester/cotton blend, it can be dyed with a fiber-reactive dye, but will turn out considerably lighter due to the polyester portion rejecting the dye. Consider the percentage of the fiber blends in your fabric before you dye.

If you are going to use a fiber-reactive dye, it is ideal to presoak your clothing in soda ash. Soda ash is a chemical called sodium carbonate that will raise the pH of the material, making the fibers more responsive to the dye. Add about a cup of soda ash per gallon of warm water. Soak your garment for up to an hour, and then wring out the excess before dyeing. Soda ash can be found anywhere that pool supplies are sold, because it is used to raise the pH of the water.

Keep personal safety in mind when using dyes and related chemicals. While some dyes are non-toxic and easy to deal with, others may be dangerous. Remember to read the manufacturer's labels for any warnings, and take the proper precautions.

COLORING

TUTORIAL

Dip-dye

Sure signs of winter include lots of time in the kitchen and snuggly wool accessories. Combining the two, we can use vinegar and a food coloring recipe to put a sunny spin on old wool. This method of dyeing can also be applied to nylon, alpaca, and other animal-derived fibers.

38

What You'll Need:

- Wool or other animal fiber garment
- White vinegar
- Water
- Microwave
- Food coloring
- Small bowls for mixing color
- Microwave-safe bowl
- Plastic bag
- Plate
- Rubber gloves

Get Prepared:

While dip-dyeing is a popular process, I'd like to show you a method that avoids using a hot stove and can be used to create a blend of shades.

Here we will be pouring dye over arm warmers that have been laid out flat to get a variegated look. You can also dye a wool garment a single color by adding a packet of food coloring to enough water to cover the garment, and zapping according to the microwave directions in Step 5. Rinse as in Step 6.

1 | **Soak in a Vinegar Bath**
Soak the garment in a bath of one part vinegar and one part water. White vinegar is necessary to lower the pH of the fabric, allowing the dye to adhere. The fiber needs to fully absorb the vinegar, so let the garment sit at least an hour before continuing. When dyeing a larger batch of clothing, allow a few hours or an overnight soak.

2 | **Prepare the Dye**
Drip food coloring into small cups of water. The water will make the dye go farther, and in this case produce a lighter pastel color instead of bold primary colors. Use two drops of food coloring per tablespoon of water, or less for pastel colors on white fabric.

3 | **Apply the Dye**
Lay a plastic bag out on a plate or tray, and fluff up the sides to create a barrier that will protect against dye spills. Lay the garment, still wet from the vinegar bath, in the center of the tray. Pour the dye over the fabric, making sure that the fabric is completely saturated. For stronger splashes of color, drip food coloring straight from the bottle onto the fabric.

4 | **Blend Colors**
Use your finger to blend colors together in spaces where there is no dye. Flip the garment over to make sure that the dye has saturated to the other side and blend there as well.

5 | Cook the Dye

Place the dyed garment in a microwave-safe bowl. Use a paper towel or plastic bag to prevent moisture from escaping during the heating process. Cook on "high" for five minutes. Remove the bowl from the microwave and let it cool completely. When cooled, flip the garment over in the bowl; this helps to heat the fiber evenly, preventing it from scorching. Return the bowl to the microwave for another five minutes.

6 | Rinse

After the dyed garment has cooled, rinse it in warm water to remove any excess dye. Add a bit of laundry detergent, rinse again, and hang to dry.

COLORING

TUTORIAL

Spraying

Spraying dye and paints can saturate a material or give it a busy pattern of tiny specks. It is common to spray dye on fabric, but there is a special trick to coloring leather.

What You'll Need:

- Leather shoes or other accessory
- 99% isopropyl alcohol or acetone
- Reinforcement stickers
- Masking tape
- Stickers
- Black leather paint
- Spray bottle
- Paintbrush
- Matte acrylic varnish
- Paper towel or cotton balls
- Sheet of paper

Get Prepared:

Isopropyl alcohol and acetone nail polish remover are less caustic than professional grade leather finish remover, but care should still be taken to avoid inhaling them. Leather paints, finish remover, and varnish can be found in some craft stores, cobbler shops, and online. As with any paint or varnish, always work in a well-ventilated area.

1 | Tape Everything Else

On heels, there are often wood, plastic, or even cork parts that you might not want speckled with paint. Use masking tape to cover any area that you do not want to paint.

2 | Remove the Varnish

Leather shoes have a clear finish on them to protect from wear and fading. We need to remove it in order to recolor the leather. Use a piece of paper towel or some cotton balls to apply the rubbing alcohol or acetone. You will need to do a lot of rubbing to get the finish off; work on the leather until it is no longer shiny. Wait about 15 minutes for the alcohol to evaporate completely.

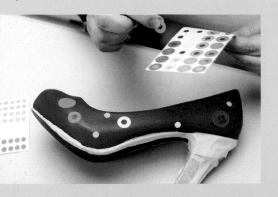

3 | Apply Stickers

Use the stickers to block out parts of the piece. To make them easier to peel up, layer two stickers in each spot.

4 | Spray with Leather Paint

Leather paint can sometimes be found in a spray form, but often you will need to put it into your own spray bottle. Test the spray on a sheet of paper, and water down the paint until it sprays easily. A thick paint will only crack and peel as the shoe is worn. Spray with care, making sure not to oversaturate the stickers. Soaking them will make them harder to get off.

5 | Flicking Paint

You can also flick the paint on with a paintbrush. If you are looking for just a few more speckles, for example, tap a loaded paintbrush against the palm of your hand to cover a smaller area. With this method, you can dab paint around the stickers with a sponge brush so that they are well covered but not oversaturated. Then add your speckles for a sprayed look.

6 | Remove the Stickers

Before the paint is dry, carefully peel away the stickers. Use a pin to catch the edge of a sticker if it is difficult to remove. Carefully bend the piece to flex the leather. This will help to stretch the leather and keep the paint from cracking during the drying process. Let the paint dry for at least eight hours.

7 | Apply Varnish

Spray the shoes with an acrylic varnish to protect your new paint job from weather and wear. Hold the heel of the pump and bend it again to prevent paint cracking. Allow them to dry completely, then add another coat of varnish and give them another stretch. Let them dry completely before wearing.

COLORING

(TUTORIAL)

Tie-dye

Tie-dyeing can be traced back to ancient China, yet has become synonymous with hippie style since the 1960s. While it is often associated with the Technicolor explosions mingling on Grateful Dead t-shirts, there is more to this art than consecutive circles.

What You'll Need:

- Cotton/cotton blend garment
- Soda ash solution in water
- Black fiber-reactive dye
- Rubber bands
- Rubber gloves
- Plastic bag
- Sink/tub

Get Prepared:

A fiber-reactive dye can easily be purchased in powdered form, as black tie-dye sold in squirt bottles or in packets that can be put into empty ketchup bottles. Be sure to cover any surface that you are not willing to stain black, or work outside if possible. Wear rubber gloves to prevent staining your hands, and presoak your garment in a soda ash solution (as described on page 37) for the best results.

We are going to use an accordion-folding technique to change a plain white garment into an edgy, patterned piece.

1 | **Fold the Garment**
Fold your piece lengthwise in half. Fold an inch-wide section forward, then back on itself. Repeat this accordion-style of folding until you have a stack of folds.

2 | **Add Rubber Bands**
Strap on rubber bands, wrapping them two or three times to make a tight hold. Add the bands to the middle and ends first to hold your folded pattern as you add more bands.

3 | **Saturate the Fabric**
Coat the gathered area in dye. For more color, completely saturate the leggings. If the dye does not penetrate the fabric, you will have more white areas than black.

4 | **Set the Dye**
Let the dye set for at least eight hours. Wrap your work in a plastic bag so that it does not dry out while the dye is setting.

5 | **Rinse and Open**
Use warm water to get all of the dye out of the garment. Rinse until the water runs clear. Remove the rubber bands to reveal the tie-dyed pattern. Let the piece dry completely before wearing.

Five Ways to Tie-Dye a T-shirt

You can achieve a variety of patterns by tying the clothes in specific ways before dyeing. Here are five examples of tie techniques:

Starburst

Add rubber bands to small points of fabric pulled up all over the shirt.

Twirl

Pull up a point on the center of the shirt and twist. Add rubber bands down the stalk while the material is still twisted.

Rumpled

Bunch the fabric loosely with your hands, and then crumple the shirt into a ball. Secure the ball with a few rubber bands before applying the dye.

Target

Pull up a point on the center of the shirt. Wrap a few rubber bands down the "stalk" you have created. Each rubber band will create a circle in the target. From here, you can apply different colors in the spaces between the rubber bands.

Stripes

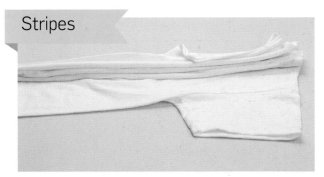

Accordion-fold a dry shirt vertically to create a thin stack of fabric. Liberally apply a stripe of dye down the middle of the fabric, avoiding the folded edges. Cover in a plastic bag, and then weigh down with books while the dye sets.

COLORING

TUTORIAL

Batik

In batik, wax is used as a resist to the dye, allowing for intricate stamped designs and high control of where the dye is applied. Batik was most famously first used on the Indonesian island of Java, where the beautifully decorated garments were restricted to the aristocratic class. These days anyone can practice batik using very inexpensive materials.

What You'll Need:

- Soy wax
- Microwave
- Fiber-reactive dye
- Rubber gloves (optional)
- Newspaper
- Copy paper
- Iron
- Ironing board
- Paintbrushes
- Foam stamps
- Hot plate (optional)
- Microwave-safe dish

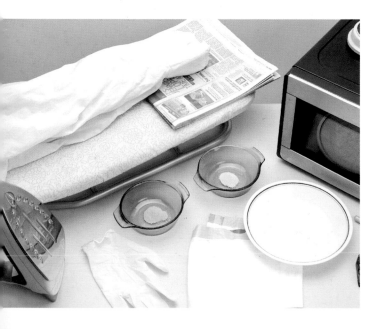

Get Prepared:

Use a fabric that will work well with fiber-reactive dye. This dye does not need to be heated to work, which is ideal when working with the hot wax. Soy wax and foam stamps offer an easy alternative to paraffin wax, with its high melting point, and the complicated copper tools used in traditional batik methods. We are going to use a microwave and easy-to-find supplies to create our batik piece.

1 | **Heat the Wax**
Soy wax is ideal because it heats at a very low temperature. It can be microwaved, which eliminates the need for a double-broiler and a lot of hassle. In a microwave-safe bowl, heat about a cup of the soy wax for two minutes.

You will need to reheat the soy wax every now and then while painting it on the garment. To avoid this, I have employed a small hot plate used for keeping coffee warm. If you use a hot plate, set it to the lowest "keep warm" setting.

2 | **Paint Designs in Wax**
Lay the fabric of the garment out flat. Use a small paintbrush to apply details like swirls, lettering, and freehand drawings. If you are unsure of your painting skills, practice first with the wax on a sheet of paper. Use light strokes of the brush to achieve a variety of line thicknesses. Rinse the paintbrush in hot water to remove the wax.

3 | **Stamp in Wax**
Foam stamps work well with soy wax. Use the paintbrush to apply wax to the stamp, and then stamp firmly onto the fabric. After making a few stamp marks, you may need to scrape dried wax from the stamp to continue to get clear prints. Stamp designs look great along hems and seam lines.

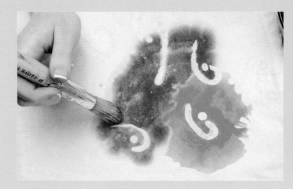

4 | Apply the Dye

Batik is recognized by the signature crackling of the resist areas. You can add this crackled effect to your garment by bunching up the waxed areas before applying the dye. Alternatively, for smooth, exact lines, be careful not to crackle the wax. This choice in the degree of crackling is yet another benefit of using soy wax.

Use a large paintbrush to apply fiber-reactive dye. Color in specific waxed areas of the garment, or let the color take on shapes, pictures, and lettering in addition to the wax. If you are looking for a single-color design, you can also don rubber gloves and dip-dye the entire garment in a tub of fiber-reactive dye. Let the dye set for at least eight hours. Use cold water to rinse out the excess dye until the water runs clear.

5 | Iron Away the Wax

Now all that is left to do is to remove the dried wax. Pick off especially large chunks of wax by hand, then use an iron and newspaper to draw the remaining wax out of the fabric. Place a thick layer of newspapers on an ironing board, and then place a clean piece of copy paper on top. The copy paper is in place so that the ink on the newspaper does not bleed onto the garment.

Lay out a single layer of the garment on top of the copy paper, and then add another piece of copy paper and a couple of pieces of newspaper on top. Set the iron to the highest non-steam setting. Iron over the top layer of newspaper until the wax bleeds through. Replace or shift the newspaper and copy paper as it becomes saturated with wax.

Batikwalla

Victoria Dresdner of Batikwalla was self-taught in all aspects of batik, with a little help from the public library. Her pieces are like paintings made with molten beeswax, hand dyed, hang dried, repainted, redyed, and finally laboriously cleaned in a cauldron of boiling water. Her designs are created spontaneously with a freehand style, but using a traditional full immersion technique. www.batikwalla.com

How did you get into batik work?

I was originally inspired by my mom's arts and craft books. I was absolutely fascinated with batik. Although I thought it would be really hard to do, I loved the effect of the crackled wax patterns on the fabric.

At age 18 I moved to Oregon and discovered a little local crafts market happening downtown every Saturday. I saw a need for radical batik designs to be sold there, and being only 18 wasn't very inhibited in the world of art expression. I had nothing to lose, so I gathered a few supplies from the University of Oregon art supply store, and experimented on a cotton bedsheet that I cut into sections. I really liked the results of my first project, which was a basic yellow, orange, and red sun, but I thought t-shirts would sell better. Up until then I had only worked summer jobs as a teenager, so my understanding of money and work was based on that. When I brought my modest collection of batik t-shirts to this little market, I almost sold out, which just blew me away. Not only did I absolutely love making batiks, but other people liked them too and they were willing to pay me for it. After that, there was no turning back. I knew that was exactly what I wanted to do from then on.

Do you plan everything out, have an inspiration board, or make it up as you go along?

All of the above! And it also depends on how many items I'm doing at a time. Since this is a business, I have to think in larger scales for building inventory, but even for specialty pieces I have a particular approach. I look at the item of clothing I'm about to work on, and I think of the placement of the design on the body and how it would work with the shape of the particular garment. I work with what I already have. For example, if it's a V-neck shirt I'll usually place the design on the shoulder, because that's more flattering to the style, as opposed to the center of the shirt, which I think would clash with the shape of the V. However, a very small detail or design can look pretty at the bottom of a V-neck. There's a song and dance to it. A boatneck shirt wouldn't be treated the same way as a scoop-neck shirt or dress.

Once I've figured out where to base my design, I have to move quickly with the wax. Mistakes happen all the time. My newest theory about mistakes is that they were meant to be, so I somehow incorporate them into the design. Sometimes I'll know what color to dye something while I'm making it, other times I wait until I can figure it out. Sometimes I take notes or draw quick sketches beforehand to really think it through. Or maybe I'll think of color combinations while I'm driving and have to jot the ideas down on a paper cup so I don't forget!

What is the most challenging part of batik dyeing?

I enjoy the technical challenges with batik and dyeing; it makes it more fun. There are some basic rules to follow with colors that are all played out well in the color wheel that we learned about in art class in elementary school. Red and blue make purple, so if you have blue fabric and dye it in red, it will come out purple. I love that! So simple and easy to understand, and so many different ways to play it. The only complaint I could make is the mess that can happen (and usually does) when dyeing and painting with molten wax. I'm more careful now than I used to be, but often I'd ruin something I was wearing when it spilled or splashed.

What number one tip would you give to someone who is just starting to work with batik?

Patience! Batik works "backwards" from our understanding of regular drawing or painting and it takes several steps. There are no shortcuts. And the dyeing is just as important as the waxing. You're going from light to dark, in layers. The fabric needs to be dry and the wax needs to be adhered to the fabric correctly (all the way through, saturating the fiber) or the effect won't show. But batik is very forgiving to mistakes with dripping beeswax. The wax makes such a lovely effect with the crackling; you could paint the simplest design and it will come out beautiful. I would recommend starting out with a very simple design, or no specific design at all, and stick to the steps. You'll be amazed in the end.

As an independent artist, how do you keep your work in the public eye?

I made my start selling at a small craft festival in southern Oregon. I was surprised at how well I did with my batiks, so I kept going. I did arts and craft fairs for a long time before selling online, so I already had a little following by the time I set up my website. Twitter and Facebook have been awesome resources for introducing my art to new people all over the world. Every time I create a new item I post it to my Facebook fan page, which automatically links the post to Twitter, and it spreads from there. I still do a few music and arts and crafts festivals and tag all my items with my biz card, so a happy customer has my info. And any interested or potential customer also gets a card so they can find me online later. They're not complicated tactics, and great ways to spread the word without too much cost or effort. I generally enjoy online communication, so it's easy for me to do.

Batik tops in Batikwalla's signature colorful style

Tie-dyed silk top by alice+olivia.

Dip-dyed dress from Internacionale.

Spray-painted shoes by Rain Blanken. See page 41.

Dip-dyed fabric necklace by Internacionale.

Tie-dyed silk maxi-dress by alice+olivia.

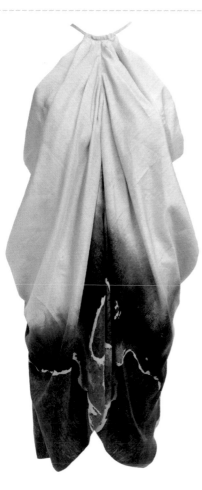

Dyed sundress from ASOS.

Rising Sun leather wallet by Jose Villar.

Dip-dyed gown from Lela Rose.

Chapter 4

PRINTING

"Isn't life a series of images that change as they repeat themselves?"

— Andy Warhol

Printed clothing has defined generations and popularized brands. The idea of replicating a design onto a wearable medium is one as old as craft itself, yet our modern methods are so advanced. From the bolts of printed fabric sold for stitching from scratch to the logo t-shirts cluttering our closets, the printed image is a commonplace occurrence in our mass-produced society.

A look back on fabric printing will take you all the way to ancient Asian countries, where block print designs were popular among artists in China and Japan. These stamped images were used alongside early screen-printing methods, which actually involved the use of human hair as the screens.

Technology advanced to allow for massive cylindrical printing plates to churn out printed fabric as early as the 1700s. Fast-forward to America in the 1960s, where Andy Warhol became the face of hand screen-printed art, and the t-shirt began to thrive as casual wear instead of an undergarment.

Technology accelerates history. In the last 20 years we have seen the invention of home inkjet printers, readily available supplies and a plethora of creativity spewing out of the internet. Hand printing never had it so good. After all, we aren't plucking our hair to make screens anymore. Now is the perfect time to get over any intimidation that home printing may have held in the past.

Printing usually involves some form of ink applied to a shirt, instead of the specialty dyes we saw in the previous chapter. Ink has a consistency that is easy to control and flows smoothly. This allows for more precise duplicates of a single image. Fabric paints can be used, and are often more cost-effective, but they tend to lie unevenly on the fabric. Decide if inks or fabric paints are best for the look you want.

Most ink is safe to handle without rubber gloves, but wear them if you are concerned about staining your skin. Also check your ink for setting instructions. Does it need to be heat-set? Should you wait a certain amount of time before machine washing? Before trying any print, remember that a scrap piece of paper can be your best friend. Always test block-print and screen-print designs on paper before you apply the design to fabric.

PRINTING

Block Print

Block printing is an easy way to stamp an image onto clothing with inks specially designed to weather wear and washing. If you can operate a stamp, you can do this.

What You'll Need:

- Slabs of rubber stamp material
- Stamp-carving tools
- Ink brayer (roller)
- Screen-print inks
- Plate or tray
- Aluminum foil
- Pencil
- Paper
- Chalk
- Towel

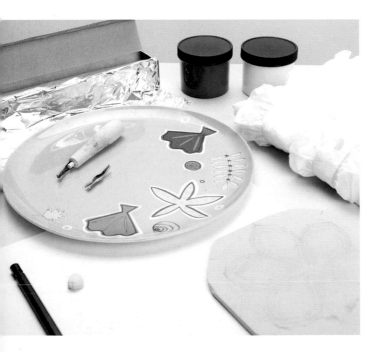

Get Prepared:

To focus on our stamp-carving skills, we are going to try a reduction block print. This will give us a multicolored image that is achieved by carving away at the same stamp in between each printing.

The rubber stamp material can be found in most craft stores, but a large eraser will work in much the same way. Just be sure to use a large, flat eraser that is thick enough to carve. Don't skimp on the stamp-carving tools. While you can get by with a hobby or craft knife, the carving tools really make this project easy. Sponged-on fabric paint can be used, but you will not get the even application that screen-print ink provides. Slide an old towel inside your garment and smooth it out before you begin. This will keep the ink from getting onto the back of the piece. Make sure there is no lint or dirt on your printing area.

1 | Draw the Design

Getting an image onto your stamp is fairly easy. Since we are doing a reduction print, the hardest part is deciding how your image will print. Moving from light colors to dark colors, how would you need to repeatedly carve away the image to achieve what you want? Play around with your pencil sketches to determine what each print will look like in each color, and what will need to be removed from the stamp with each step. If you are not skilled at freehand drawing, you can search the internet and print a design from your computer that will fit the stamp.

2 | Transfer the Design

I have made my sketch in pencil because this is the easiest way to transfer the design onto my stamp material. For printed images, trace the image in pencil before you continue. Cut a piece of stamp that is at least ¼in (5mm) bigger than your design. Lay your sketch face down on the stamp, and then rub the back of the paper with your fingernails or even the wooden handle of the stamp-carving tool. The pencil image will transfer right onto the stamp block. Before you finish, carefully peel up the paper a bit and have a peek to see if there are any spots you need to work on.

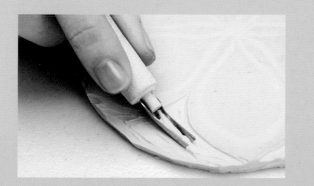

3 | Carve the Design

A typical stamp-carving tool will come with both a thick carving head and a thin one. There are specialized carving heads available, but they are not necessary for this project. Use the flat head for carving away large areas, and the thin head for carving away tight spots and detail. The first print is often a light background color, so the initial carving is usually just the surrounding border and outlines.

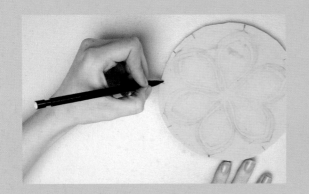

4 | ### Register the Stamp
Lay the stamp face down on the fabric. Use your pencil to make marks on the back of your stamp at the top, bottom, sides, and in between. Then, on the fabric trace with chalk around the stamp and make corresponding marks to those on the stamp. This will help to ensure that you are printing in the same spot each time.

5 | ### Application
Squeeze a bit of ink onto your plate or tray. I like to cover my plate in aluminum foil because it makes cleanup so easy ... and prevents me from ruining a plate. Roll your brayer in the ink until it is evenly coated and has a tacky feel to it. Roll the brayer onto your stamp, making sure that you have fully covered the design.

6 | ### The First Print
Hold the stamp with both hands, carefully lining it up with your registration marks before you press it onto the garment. Press around each part of the stamp to ensure a clear print. Carefully peel up the stamp. You will notice that some of the lines in the carved background have printed. This is part of the characteristic look of block printing. If you don't like these lines, you can use a paper towel to wipe excess ink from the background before printing. I am fond of the sense of movement that these lines bring, so I let them print, and even carve at them a bit here and there so that they will appear in different colors as the print progresses. Let the ink dry completely before printing another color on top. In the meantime, you can clean your stamp and brayer, and start carving the next stamp.

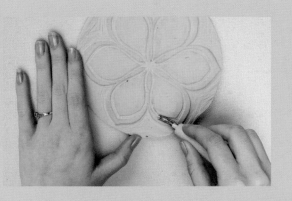

7 | Carving and Printing the Second Color

My next print will be in green, so I have carved away the extra yellow bits, registered my stamp, and printed the entire foreground image in green. Since printing inks can be pricey, I mixed yellow and blue together instead of buying a separate green ink. Continue to carve and print in this manner, reducing the printed image and using a darker ink each time.

8 | Heat-Set the Image (Optional)

Now that your multicolored image is dry, you may need to heat-set the ink. If you used fabric paint, this step is not necessary. Heat-setting the screen-printing ink is a vital step if you intend for the image to survive the washing machine. My ink calls for placing a piece of paper over the image and ironing for three to five minutes.

Add Accent Pieces

Along with your reduction-print carvings, consider adding simpler stamps to continue your color scheme. Complementary stamps can be store-bought or you can carve your own designs. I used some of the rubber corners cut away from my large flower stamp to carve these simple accents. They add a little extra interest to the dress—and ensure I get my money's worth out of the rubber material.

Heat Transfer

TUTORIAL

Heat transfers are a simple way to slap an image on any fabric that can be ironed. Many people have easy access to an inkjet printer, so these have become a popular way to quickly personalize clothing.

What You'll Need:

- Heat transfer paper
- Tissue paper
- Inkjet printer
- Scissors
- Iron and ironing board
- Pillowcase

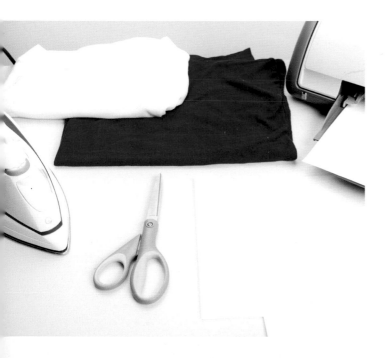

Get Prepared:

Creating a printable collage doesn't have to require a lot of Photoshop work. Here, I'd like to show you how to use heat transfer paper to transform a few everyday photos into a collage.

Public domain photos of vintage advertisements, buildings, and flowers can be found on the internet. Heat transfer paper can be found at craft stores and most major department stores. Make sure that your garment has been pre-washed and is completely dry and clean before you start.

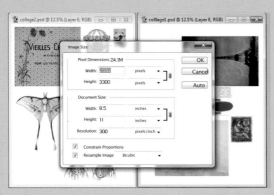

1 Prepare the Image

Heat transfer paper can be expensive, so try to fit as many images as possible onto each sheet. This tutorial will show you how to separate your subjects from the photo backgrounds in Photoshop. Create a new document that is 8½ × 11in (21.5 × 28cm) (this is the size of the heat transfer paper), then copy and paste your images into this document. Arrange these elements to maximize use of the page, making sure to leave room for the margins..

2 Test Print and Heat Transfer Print

Heat transfer paper can be costly, so let's make sure we are ready to print on it. Set your printer to a "fast draft" setting and test print using plain paper. Be sure that your image is not printing off of the page or getting cut off by the margin space, running a new test print each time until it looks right. Remove any copy paper from the printer and insert a single sheet of the heat transfer paper. Set your printer to a "high quality" setting and print on the heat transfer paper. Cut wide around each image to make separate pieces of paper.

3 Cut and Peel the Backing

The backing on the transfer paper can be tough to peel away from cut images, and picking at the paper can sometimes ruin the edges of your design. My trick to avoid this is to first cut a large space around each image, and then pick the backing away in a space that will be cut away from the image before ironing. Peel the backing toward the image until just a bit of it is peeled away from directly behind the print. Cut the image like you normally would, but now you have a little tab on the back to make peeling easier later.

4 | **Precision Cutting**
Use a small pair of scissors to cut out all the small details. You can also try using a hole punch or decorative scissors to build some interesting textures.

5 | **Arrange the Images**
Lay your garment on top of the pillowcase and begin arranging your cut images. Try a few different configurations, working with the shape of the garment to create your scene.

6 | **Iron the Image**
Tissue paper is required so that the iron does not melt through the plastic heat transfer. Lay the tissue paper on top of the image, taking care to cover all of the transfer paper. If your design is too big, lay an extra sheet, or iron in patches. Set the temperature of your iron according to the paper manufacturer's instructions. Usually, these papers call for firm pressure on the highest non-steam setting and there should be no water in the iron.

7 | **Check Your Work**
Check to make sure that the image is not peeling up in any areas. An image that peels up may not have been ironed enough. Replace the tissue paper and press again until you get a good stick. Avoid repressing areas that have already adhered well.

TUTORIAL   Digital Print

Digital print fabric used to be restricted to large manufacturing plants, but inkjet printers and the right fabric treatment have brought digital printing into the home. Crafters can now print directly from computer to fabric, creating detailed appliqués and patterned swatches.

What You'll Need:

- **Dress**
- **Inkjet printer**
- **White fabric**
- **Freezer paper**
- **Sheet of copy paper**
- **Bowl**
- **Wash soda**
- **Fabric softener**
- **Alum embroidery thread**
- **Needle**
- **Iron and ironing board**
- **Embroidery hoop or sewing machine**

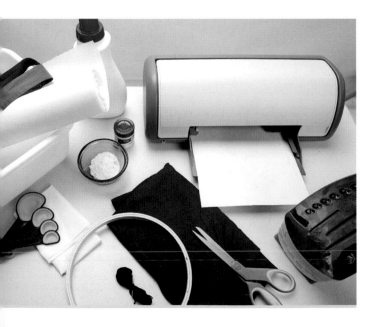

Get Prepared:

With digital printing, and some Ink-Stick solution, I can make my own printed appliqués. This method of fabric treatment can also be used to preserve ink drawings, like the Drink Me bottle at the strap of the dress I made here.

Take care when using alum; it is a caustic material and you should avoid inhaling it. The alum will begin to damage the fabric over time, so try to soak, print, and rinse the fabric over the course of a few hours to prevent corrosion. Our Ink-Stick solution is a homemade alternative to the commercially-available Bubble Jet Set fabric treatment.

1 | **Mix the Ink-Stick**
Mix the Ink-Stick using the following recipe:
1 cup hot water
$2^{1}/_{2}$ tsp wash soda
$^{3}/_{4}$ tsp fabric softener
2 tbs alum

2 | **Soak the Fabric**
Completely submerge the fabric in the Ink-Stick mixture for 10 minutes. Hang it to dry or place it in front of a cool fan to expedite the drying process.

3 | **Iron Fabric to Freezer Paper**
When your fabric is completely dry, you will need to adhere it to something sturdy that will carry it through the printer. Adjust the iron to the highest non-steam setting. Iron the fabric to a piece of freezer paper that is at least $9^{1}/_{2} \times 12$in (24 × 30cm).

4 | **Cut the Freezer Paper and Fabric**
Use a sheet of copy paper as a template to cut your fabric and freezer paper to $8^{1}/_{2} \times 11$in (21.5 × 28cm). This is an acceptable size for most inkjet printers. It is also possible to change your print settings to accept longer sheets of paper, such as legal size.

5 | **Print and Rinse the Fabric**
You can grab a few images from the internet and arrange them in Photoshop to print on a single sheet, just like in our Heat Transfer project on page 63. Print on the highest quality ink setting. After printing, let the ink set for at least half an hour, then remove the freezer paper backing and give the fabric a quick rinse in warm water to remove any excess ink.

6 | **Cut Out and Stitch the Images**
Stitch dry, printed fabric anywhere to your garment by attaching an embroidery hoop and using a tight whipstitch, hand-turned appliqué method (see page 108), or setting a sewing machine to a tight zigzag stitch. I added ribbon roses to the bottom of the skirt, as in our Ribbons tutorial on page 91, and a tiny bow on the Drink Me bottle.

7 | **Iron-On the Images**
For a no-sew solution, try turning your printed fabric into iron-on designs. At most craft stores you can find iron-on adhesive that can be applied to the back of your printed fabric. Directions vary on these products, so follow the manufacturer's instructions carefully.

Special Effect Inks

Standard screen printing ink serves as a good introduction to mixing colors and working with the consistency of inks. But when flat colors no longer satisfy your creative monster, move on to special effect inks which alter the color, texture, and tone of your print. Color effect inks are available in glow-in-the-dark, neon, and UV light change. Texture effect inks add dimension to the garment, and can include flocking (fuzzy), vinyl, and 3D puff inks. Effect inks that can transform your print into glitz and whimsy include metallic glitter, foil, and clear shimmers. These inks can require specialty chemicals, printed glues, and hot treatments, which can be difficult to achieve at home without specific equipment. Check the Resources for professional custom printers that can add these designs to your prints.

PRINTING

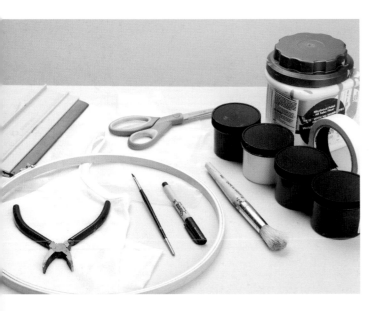

TUTORIAL

Screen Print

Popularized as an ideal way to print wallpaper in the eighteenth century, screen print is now best known for t-shirt designs. Screen printing usually involves a lot of expensive specialty supplies such as emulsion, frames, and screen material. However, those new to printing or low on cash can opt to use an embroidery hoop and latex paint to create a durable print screen.

What You'll Need:

- Sheer synthetic fabric
- Large embroidery hoop
- Pliers
- Latex house paint
- Masking tape
- Paintbrushes
- Screen-print ink
- Squeegee
- Iron
- Ironing board
- Fine-tip marker
- Cardboard insert
- Paper

Get Prepared:

The first print screens in ancient Japan were actually made of human hair, but I promise that isn't in the list of materials here. A sheer curtain works really well as an affordable printing screen, and a little goes a long way. Embroidery hoops can be found at the fabric store, and cost just a few dollars, and half-gallons of mistinted latex paint can be found on discount. These easily found materials make this an economical project, so don't skimp on the ink. Fabric paint can work with this method, but quality screen-print ink really is worth the investment. As with any paint or varnish, always work in a well-ventilated area.

1 | Assemble the Screen

Cut a piece of sheer fabric and fit it into the embroidery hoop. For hoops with an adjustable knob, it is important that you use a pair of pliers to tighten the outer hoop as much as possible. If the fabric puckers, tug it here and there as you adjust the hoop for a tight-as-a-drum fit.

2 | Trace the Design onto the Screen

Choose a design that is only as detailed as you are willing to work with. Prints with a lot of letters and intricate details can be achieved with this method, but you will need to spend more time preparing the screen. Use a fine-tip marker to trace the design onto the screen.

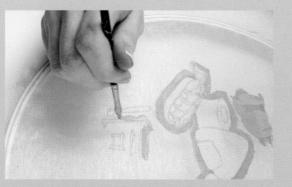

3 | Paint the Non-print Surface

We are going to use latex paint to fill in the part of the image that will not print. This is a time-consuming process, but will yield a screen that will last through hundreds of prints. I have tested a lot of different fillers, and I have found that latex paint is the best for hoop printing. It can be applied precisely to detailed images, and will last through a multitude of rinses without absorbing water. Use a small brush first to outline the design, and then use a large brush to fill in the large areas.

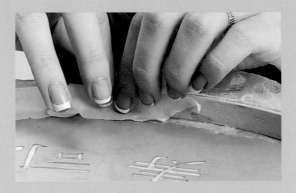

4 | Add Masking Tape to the Screen

Once the screen is dry, add masking tape around the inside edge of the screen. This will prevent ink from leaking out at the edges. Position the tape so that it is between the hoop and the screen, as shown above.

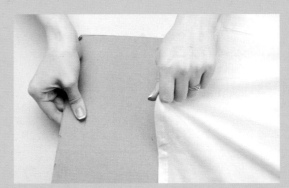

5 | Check the Screen for Pinholes

While you are applying the masking tape, keep an eye out for pinholes. These are caused by places that were missed by the paintbrush or where the paint tightened during the drying process. Hold the screen up to a light to check for pinholes. Use a small paintbrush to fill in each of these specks, using just a dot of paint. Let the screen dry completely.

6 | Prepare the Garment

Wrinkles in your garment can cause gaps in the print, so iron it first if needed. Insert a piece of cardboard into the garment so that the design is printed on a smooth surface, and does not bleed through to the back. Before you print, make sure that you are ready to work in an area that is protected from ink spills.

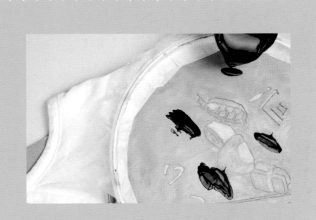

7 | Apply Ink to the Screen

The amount of ink you apply depends on how large your design is. Test your print out on paper before applying it to a piece of clothing. Examine this test print for pinholes, ink leaking on the edges, or the need for more or less ink. If you are using a small design in a large hoop, it is possible to apply the ink at the top of the screen to be pulled straight down over the image, just as in traditional print screens. When working with a larger image that fills the hoop, you will be rotating the squeegee instead. For this, evenly space ink blobs around the hoop. Only apply blobs of ink on areas that are filled with paint.

8 | Pull the Ink

Apply a squeegee at a 45-degree angle and pull the ink over the screen. Rotate the squeegee in one direction for designs that fill the screen. Pull the squeegee straight toward you for small designs in the middle of a big screen.

9 | **Reveal and Dry the Print**
Carefully lift the screen up and away from the garment without scraping it over the fabric. Let the ink dry completely. Dry time can depend on the brand of ink and humidity in the room; 20 minutes is a good rule of thumb.

10 | **Set the Ink**
Screen-print ink needs to be heated in order to become permanent and washfast. If you used fabric paint, you can skip this step. Follow the directions on your ink for setting. This usually involves ironing for five minutes with a sheet of paper between the iron and the ink.

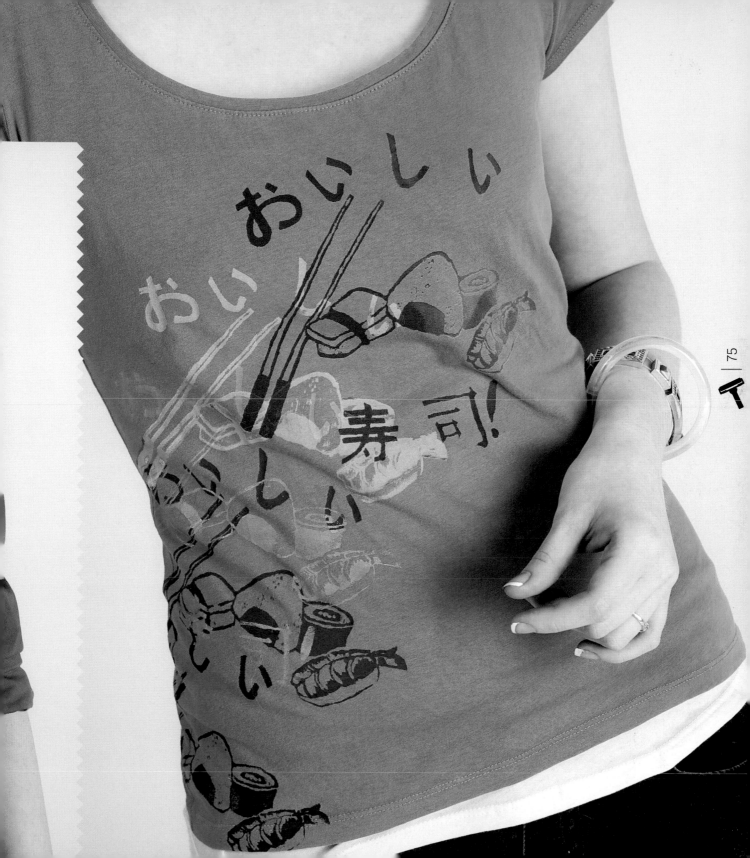

PRINTING

TUTORIAL

Pen and Ink

Freehand designs on clothing are one of the most personal forms of expression we can wear. From graffiti pumps to signature t-shirts, these one-of-a-kind designs are quintessentially handmade—fingers to fabric.

What You'll Need:

- **Plant-fiber or silk garment**
- **Permanent ink pens**
- **Cardboard**
- **Ink-Stick solution**
- **Iron and ironing board**
- **Copy paper**

Get Prepared:

Permanent markers are easy to find and are famous for working well on canvas shoes. Here I am going to show you how to pre-treat and finish a garment so that you can uncap the same creative spirit from head to toe. I used a black-and-white dress for this project, but you can also go for lightly-colored garments that will mix well with the permanent ink pens. The only stipulation here is to stick to plant-derived fabrics and silks, which will do a good job of holding onto the ink.

1 | Pretreat the Fabric
Soak your garment in the Ink-Stick recipe provided on page 67. Let the garment dry with a cool fan; avoid exposing it to excessive heat or sun, as these will accelerate the corrosive properties of the alum.

2 | Insert Cardboard
Insert a large piece of cardboard to protect the back side of your garment and work surface. Avoid using smooth or plastic inserts and work surfaces; the ink may get on these and smudge to other parts of the dress if the fabric shifts.

3 | Begin Coloring
Apply color evenly to the fabric, and avoid oversaturation. Too much ink could bleed later in the wash. If there is an existing design on your garment, try to work with it to create interesting accents.

4 | Mixing and Setting Color
To build depth and texture in your design, try crosshatching or stippling with the pens. This is a great way to mix colors, and will give the fabric a different effect when viewed far away or close-up.

Optional Tips for Lasting Images

Your garment can be worn and washed after coloring, but here are some hints to make your work last longer.

Half an hour after the ink has dried, dunk the garment in cold water for a light rinse. You will lose a bit of the ink color during this process, but it is an important precursor for setting the ink. To set the ink, let the fabric dry completely, and then iron the inked areas for three to five minutes with a piece of blank copy paper between the iron and the garment.

Wait a week before machine washing the garment for the first time, and always avoid a hot water wash. Lighter inks will wash and fade first, and will appear to last longer if used to fill large areas of color. Signatures and fine line art will last better through repeated washings if done in dark purple, brown, or black.

Using Carbon Paper

You don't have to be artistically gifted to create cool ink customizations. If you have any line art that you would like to transfer onto a garment, employ the use of carbon paper. This special paper will duplicate any image you trace over it (check out how we used it to create a pattern for the Punch Needle technique on page 150). Position the carbon paper between a page of line art and the garment. Work on a flat surface and pin or tape the pages in place to keep them from shifting. Trace the line art, being careful not to rest your hand on the paper. The pressure of your pen will transfer the image to the garment, and voila, you're an artist.

Great sources for line art:

- Coloring book pages
- Google image search for clipart
- Newspapers and magazines
- Scrapbook paper patterns

80

Screendream

Daniella Trigo of Screendream produces handmade silk-screen prints on fabrics and clothing in one-off pieces or in extra-small runs. She mixes traditional silk screening with contemporary processes and eco-friendly textile inks to embellish all types of fabric surfaces. Creative screen printing and inimitable bespoke print designs make Screendream's work truly one of a kind. www.etsy.com/shop/screendream

How did you get into screen printing?

In my first year at design school I ended up making prints in all my sketchbooks and projects, so I decided to specialize in print design for fashion. That's when I started screen printing and loved it. I've done different types of printing but the whole process of screen printing is what I most like.

What kinds of art or experiences have influenced your printed designs?

I think art deco and its geometric aesthetic come through in my printed designs; I like to play with shapes and a clean graphic style. I also like to use personal experiences to make prints; I've done prints about broken hearts and trying new foods. I look to things around me or close to me for inspiration, from ironwork on the houses in my neighborhood to a pair of strappy sandals or my grandma's cut-glass liquor bottles. When I do prints for clients, I think about them and their environment and include some personal aspects in the design.

How do you decide which design would make a good print?

I start with an idea and gather images that relate to it: photographs, drawings, objects, anything to translate the idea in my head into something visual. Then I make some key elements like shapes or textures that fit into the idea, and play with them to build the print design. From this point the design starts happening almost on its own; the shapes tell me where to go with a print and new visual ideas appear and develop. The final print might even be far from the original idea, but if it works visually, I think it makes a good print. I think a good print can be made from anything, as long as it works visually or conceptually, and is interesting through the shapes, textures, colors, and arrangement of all these elements.

What is the most challenging aspect of screen printing?

One of the technical challenges I face is deciding which technique to use for each print design and for the fabric I'm using. The print technique should convey the idea or feel of each print, whether it is a light, transparent look, something quite opaque and heavy, devoré cutouts, or a vintage discharge.

What number one, can't-live-without tip would you give to someone who is just starting to screen print?

Always do tests with colors and fabrics to get everything right before you do an entire print run. Although there are guidelines, tests are always useful! It's also useful to do wash tests to make sure the fabric holds the ink well. In general, it's better to do lots of preparation and testing beforehand to minimize mishaps.

As an independent artist, how do you keep your work in the public eye?

I sell in local shops and markets, and friends and clients spread the word about my work. I sometimes use Facebook to advertise new items or to let people know where they can buy my work, and I send out promotional emails. I also get together with other designers every so often to do special sale events or "pop-up" shops.

Top left and right: Daniella Trigo makes schematic images of garments prior to printing (top left). This allows her to balance out the colors and prints for each collection (right). **Below:** Decanters pattern.

Block-printed jacket from Monsoon.

Digital print silk dress from French Connection.

Fashion Mob t-shirt print by Bora Aksu for People Tree.

Long Pia Dress in Dusk digital print by Zero + Maria Cornejo.

Digital print dress by Mary Katrantzou.

Handpainted caps, wallet, and shoes by Bobsmade.

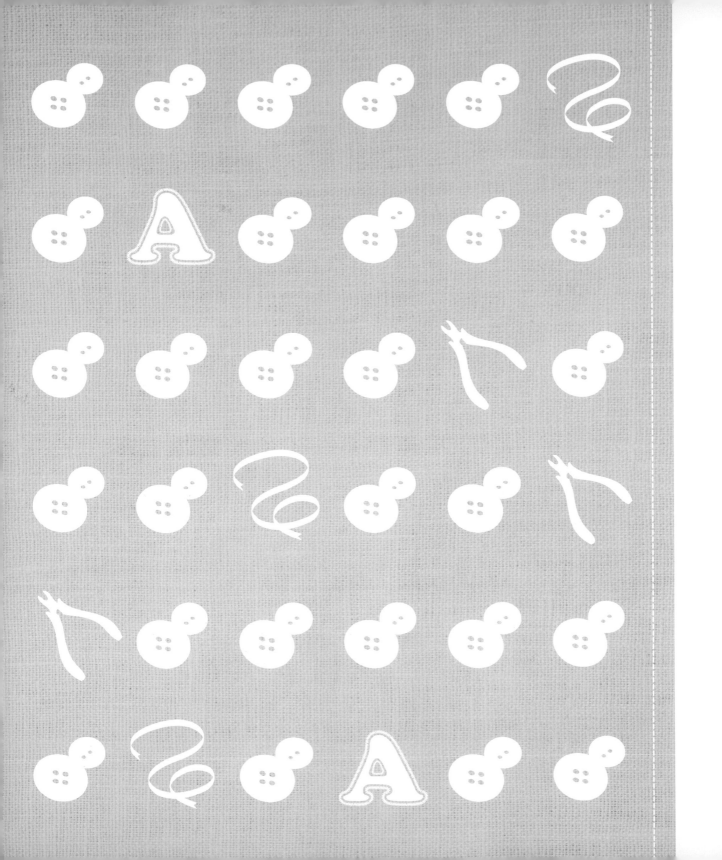

Chapter 5 |

EMBELLISHMENTS

"In order to be irreplaceable, one must always be different."

— Coco Chanel

While dyeing and printing will change the color of clothing, embellishments actually add foreign material to the design. With embellishments we can create shine and glitter with beads and sequins, or soft raised textures with ribbon and lace. Everyone needs at least one beaded top or cute buttoned cardigan. It is hard to imagine fashion without these extras.

Embellishments are a very strong element of design, so they tend to rotate very quickly in and out of fashion. While some trendy looks will lose their flavor entirely, timeless pieces will continue to endure for years. This happens both in the world of fashion and in the world of my closet.

I think of Coco's wise words every time I open a closet full of clothes that I don't want to wear. It seems that each of my embellished garments resides in one of two designated areas of the closet: Things I Hate Now and Things I'll Hate Later. What do they have in common? I'll never get rid of them!

The beaded favorites of today are sure to make me cringe six months from now. In turn, an embroidered skirt I love will most likely find its way to the back of the closet before next spring. But I just can't seem to get rid of that sequined top … I might need something flashy one day. Embellished garments are just as Coco said … they are all different, and they all have an important place in my wardrobe. Whether I love or hate them at the moment, they still haven't made the thrift store cut.

Stitching on a few ribbon flowers, buttons, and bows can take a plain shirt to the next level. The quick addition of patches, buttons, or baubles can really add interest to your wardrobe. It is also most often an inexpensive venture, making it a cheap way to upgrade garments that may have been on their way out.

Control the power of your embellished pieces by pairing them with clothing that does not "compete" with them. Accents like beads and patches can "take over" a look, creating centerpieces that would be better paired with coordinating shoes and accessories instead of a lot of crazy patterns or other embellished clothing.

EMBELLISHMENTS

TUTORIAL

Sequins

Today's plastic sequins originate from the ancient practice of stitching gold coins to clothing as a sign of abundant wealth. The glamour-power of sequins is still in full effect, adding an instant glimmer of luxury to any outfit.

What You'll Need:

- Sequins
- Small beads
- Sheer fabric
- Needle
- Thread
- Small beads
- Scissors
- Fabric glue

Get Prepared:

Use a sheer fabric such as organza or tulle as a base for your sequin work. If your sequin doesn't make a bowl shape, then it is upside-down. Always thread sequins so that the curved, glittering side is facing up.

1 | **Running Sequins**
Thread the needle with at least 12in (30cm) of thread. Start stitching from the inside of the hat so that the thread knot is concealed. Stitch a couple of times to anchor the thread onto the hat. Thread a sequin onto the needle. Press the sequin flat on the fabric.

Insert the needle into the fabric, slightly to the left or right of the front edge of the sequin, as shown. Push the needle to emerge again directly in front of the sequin. Thread another sequin, effectively hiding the stitches placed on the first sequin. Repeat this process all the way around the hat, rethreading the needle when necessary.

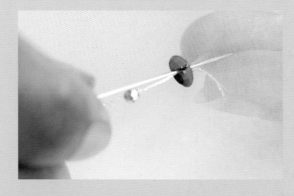

2 | **Beaded Sequins**
Beads can be used to anchor sequins, which is a great way to create "floating" sequins that do not appear to have any surrounding stitches. Here, I used beaded sequins as the base of the design worked on sheer fabric. Bring the needle up through the sheer fabric.

To do this, thread on a sequin and a small bead, settling them into place on the fabric. Insert the needle into the center of the sequin and through to the other side of the fabric. This will secure the bead to the center of the sequin. Repeat this simple process to create a cluster of beaded sequins.

3 | Cut Out the Sequin Work
I worked groups of beaded sequins and running sequins to create a simple flower design, but you can expand on this idea to create lots of little flowers, animals, or abstract shapes for your piece. Cut out your designs with care, minding the edge of the fabric so that it is trimmed behind the sequins. If your sheer fabric has a low thread count, you may want to apply a permanent fabric glue to prevent the fabric from fraying.

4 | Stitch the Sequin Work to the Piece
Stitch the sheer fabric to the hat using a matching thread. Since the fabric is trimmed so close to the edges of the sequins, you will need to stitch very close to the sequins, or in an open area of fabric like the petals on the sequined flower (see above).

TUTORIAL Ribbons

There is more to ribbon than wrapping packages and trimming garments. Ribbon can be manipulated in endless ways to create a variety of beautiful fabric flowers.

What You'll Need:

- Ribbon
- Tulle
- Beads
- Rickrack
- Scrap satin or organza fabric
- Seam-sealer glue
- Measuring tape
- Needle
- Straight pins
- Thread
- Scissors
- Iron and ironing board
- Sewing machine (optional)

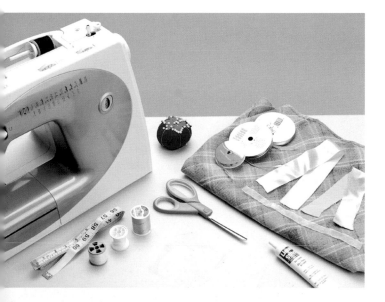

Get Prepared:

Let's try seven different ways to turn ribbon into a blooming summer garden. Each method uses just a little bit of ribbon, so this project can be completed even if you are working with scraps.

Take your time when choosing the colors and textures of your ribbons. For a soft look, we have chosen a lot of neutral tones with bright splashes of color. Use a garment with a thicker weave to help support the bulk of the stitched embellishments. If your ribbon unravels easily, apply seam sealer to all of the raw edges and let them dry completely.

Frayed Satin Roses

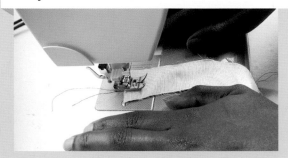

1 | Cut a 4in (10cm) square piece of tulle to use as the base for this flower. Cut a 12in (30cm) strip of scrap satin or organza. Position the edge of the ribbon in the center of the tulle, letting the rest of the ribbon hang loose. Backstitch the middle of the ribbon to the tulle (use the backstitch setting on a sewing machine, or see page 140 for instructions on how to backstitch by hand).

2 | Straight-stitch down the middle of the ribbon, turning the tulle square as you stitch. The ribbon will begin to curl in a spiral, and the raw edges will start to stand up. Stitch until you are out of ribbon, or until your rose reaches the desired size.

3 | You can clip the extra tulle away from the rose, or even leave it to add more gentle texture to your garment.

Sheer Lily Petals

1 Cut a 4in (10cm) piece of 1in (2.5cm) wide ribbon. Fold the middle of the ribbon at a 90-degree angle.

2 Touch the two ends of the ribbon together so that the middle fold naturally forms a point.

3 Pinch the ribbon in half lengthwise. String the loose edges of the folded ribbon onto a threaded needle. Repeat these steps four more times so that you have five petals poised on the needle.

4 Pull the needle through all five of the folded petals to gather them at the center. Crisscross stitches at the bottom to secure. Knot the thread and snip, or use the extra thread to go ahead and sew the lily to the skirt.

Flat-stitched Roses

1 Thin ribbon can be stitched directly onto the skirt to create pictures of flowers. To make a rose, stitch ½in (1cm) of the ribbon to the skirt, then fold the ribbon through 90 degrees. Continue to stitch over the fold and another ½in (1cm) length of ribbon, then fold again to create a boxy circle.

2 When your circle is complete, continue to create the rose by starting another angular circle inside the last. You can overlap portions of the circles or keep them far apart for a stylized look. Make as many circles as it takes to reach the center of the rose. Clip the ribbon and fold over the end of the rose. Stitch this folded portion to the middle of the rose. Knot the thread and clip on the inside of the skirt.

Chubby Layered Rosebuds

1 | Cut a 6in (15cm) length of 2in (5cm) wide satin ribbon. Fold the ribbon lengthwise, right sides together, and iron it. Fold the edges of the ribbon back toward the fold and iron again to achieve this accordion fold.

2 | We are going to stitch together the edges and center fold of the ribbon to allow our accordion folds to pop out. Use a matching thread to straight-stitch all the way across the ribbon. Pull the thread to gather into a flower shape.

3 | Stitch through all of the layers of fabric in one direction, then the other, and knot. This crisscross pattern will secure the bottom of the flower. Snip the thread, or keep it attached to go ahead and sew the flower onto the garment. Apply seam sealer to prevent the raw edges of the ribbon from unraveling.

Tiny Gathered Carnations

1 | For a wisp of a carnation, use a sheer ½in (1cm) wide ribbon. Work from left to right. Fold the end of the ribbon in ¼in (5mm), and then fold ¼in (5mm) of the ribbon to the left directly over the first fold. Continue this pattern, stacking ¼in (5mm) at a time as shown. Use a straight pin to hold the folds together as you work.

2 | Stitch the folds together with matching thread, working as close to the edge of the ribbon as possible.

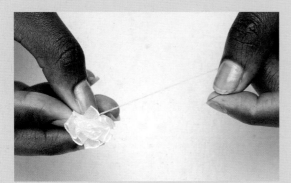

3 | Pull the thread, gathering the folded ribbon together to form the flower. Stitch through the gathered area in one direction, and then the other, crisscrossing to secure the bottom of the flower.

Delicate Beaded Daisies

1 | This look works well with thin ribbon, but can be used with thick types as well. Pierce the end of the ribbon with a threaded needle. Create a loop as large as you want the petals to be. Skewer the end of the loop onto the needle. Repeat, creating as many loops of ribbon as you care to add. Add a bead to the needle tip, then pull the needle through. Push the needle back through the hole it emerged from. Knot the thread at the back of the flower. Snip the extra thread, or go ahead and sew the flower to the skirt.

Green Rickrack Stems

1 | Wavy rickrack is perfect for ready-made stems. Straight-stitch the rickrack onto the skirt with a matching thread color. Weave it in and out of the placed flowers to give the impression of stem greenery. It can help to first pin the rickrack to the skirt while you plot out the design.

TUTORIAL Beads

Glass, plastic, wood, metal, and more. If it has a hole in it, any bead can elevate plain clothing to the heights of texture and interest. The kind of beads you apply can change the entire tone of any garment, adding a flash of sparkle or elegance.

What You'll Need:

- Beads of varying sizes and colors
- Freezer paper
- Fusible interfacing
- Needle
- Thread
- Pencil
- Scissors
- Masking tape
- Tweezers
- Iron and ironing board

Get Prepared:

Beads are like little jewels, so let's treat them as such with the proper stitching and fabric preparation. I'll show you how to use fusible interfacing to create a strong design, and how to put freezer paper to work as a bead map.

Be sure to use beads that will fit over the eye of your needle. For smaller seed beads, use a needle specially made for beading that is strong enough to guide through the fabric of your garment.

1 | **Sketch the Beaded Area on Freezer Paper**
Take a look at your garment and decide where you would like to add beads. Along the collar, and near the buttons and cuffs of sleeves are great areas for beading. Trace the area to be beaded on a piece of freezer paper. This paper is going to come in handy later as a map of your design. Cut out the freezer paper pieces.

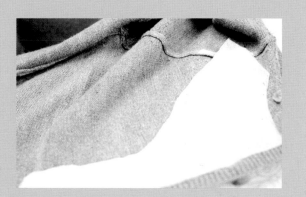

2 | **Use Freezer Paper to Cut the Interfacing**
We are going to use interfacing to help strengthen the fabric and keep it from wrinkling or puckering while we stitch the beads. Use the freezer paper pieces as templates for corresponding interfacing pieces. Trace the freezer paper onto a sheet of interfacing, and cut it out.

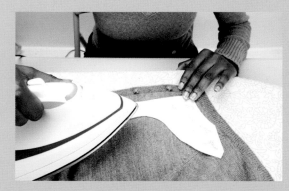

3 | **Iron the Freezer Paper to the Garment**
Set the iron to the hottest non-steam setting and iron the freezer paper to the front of the garment. It should only take a minute or so to get the paper to stick.

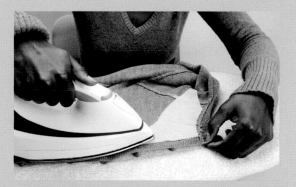

4 | **Iron the Interfacing to the Garment**
Turn the garment inside out. Iron the interfacing to the inside of the fabric, being careful to line these pieces up with the mirror-image freezer paper on the other side of the fabric.

5 | Sketch the Beadwork Design

Use a pencil to sketch the bead design right onto the freezer paper. Use the beads themselves as guides to shape and size. Write in symbols for similar beads so that you do not get confused, like "S," "M," and "L" for size or special characters to represent the color or type of bead. Keep a "key" on hand that explains the meaning of each symbol.

6 | Organize Beads on Masking Tape

A great way to keep track of your beads is to stick them to a piece of masking tape. Organize groups of beads so that they are ready to be stitched on together.

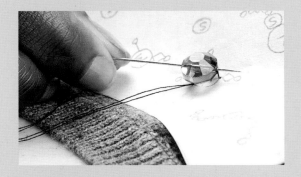

7 | Stitch on Large Beads

To stitch on large beads, first insert your threaded needle in through the back of the garment. Stitch twice to anchor the thread (do this where the bead will cover these stitches). Come up from the back of the fabric and thread the bead. Insert the needle back into the fabric, moving underneath the bead and out again to make another pass through the bead. This method of double-stitching will help to ensure that large beads stay put.

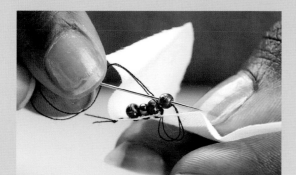

8 | Stitch on Small Beads

Smaller beads work best when the thread is "woven" through to connect them. With the thread coming up out of the right side of the fabric, thread a small bead onto the needle. Insert the needle into the fabric directly in front of the bead. Bring the needle back up behind the bead and through the bead hole again. This time, add the next bead to the needle. Stitch the bead to the fabric by inserting the needle directly in front of it. As before, come up behind the bead. Repeat to create a neat line of small beads.

9 | Peel Away the Freezer Paper

Once your beads are all in place, gently peel the freezer paper away from the front of the garment. Use a pair of tweezers to remove spots of paper from underneath the bead clusters. Once you have beaded a piece of clothing, you will need to take extra care when washing it. Consider hand washing beaded pieces.

TUTORIAL

Studs

Studs are a staple of biker gear and seem to recur every few years in high fashion. Depending on their use, they can add an edgy toughness or simply a metallic glimmer to your clothes. One way to add geeky style to an old article of clothing is to use square studs as pixels.

102

What You'll Need:

- Studs
- Sandpaper
- Acrylic paints
- Sponge brush
- Matte acrylic finish spray
- Chalk
- Measuring tape
- Pliers

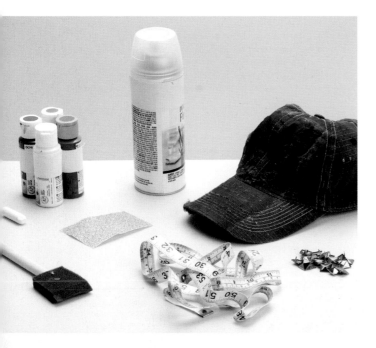

Get Prepared:

The ¹⁄₂in (1cm) silver and gold studs that I used for this tutorial can be harvested from an old studded belt or purchased at a craft store. Studs in assorted colors are harder to find, so it is often easier to paint metallic studs. You can also use iron-on studs, but I have found that these are prone to falling off over time. I upcycled an old baseball cap for this project, which first had to be darned using the method found on page 132.

1 | **Sand the Studs**
Studs are a smooth metal, so we need to scratch them up a bit to get our paint to stick. Lightly rub the sandpaper over the surface of the stud until you can see a good crosshatch pattern.

2 | **Paint the Studs**
A sponge brush will give you good, even coverage on these studs. Apply two coats of paint, allowing them to dry fully between each coat (allow at least one to two hours).

3 | **Apply a Matte Finish**
To protect the paint from scratching or fading, spray the studs once with a matte acrylic finishing spray. The studs absolutely will not hold the paint unless protected.

4 | **Chalk it Out**
Measure and chalk out an area to apply the studs. You can also take this opportunity to paint or dye this area to liven up your design.

5 | Apply Studs to the Garment

Line up the stud with your chalked line. Push the prongs of the stud through the material, then use your pliers to push the prongs back toward the middle of the stud. Take a look at the inside of the piece to make sure that the stud is not bunching the fabric. Bunching can happen if the prongs on the stud are not straight, or if the fabric wrinkled prior to insertion. Remove any studs that are pulling at the material, straighten the prongs and fabric, and reapply.

6 | Apply Studs to a Hat Brim

Place studs on the brim of a hat by stabbing the prong of the stud in sideways. Bend the other prong at a 45-degree angle and use your pliers to help push the prong in as you flatten the stud onto the hat. On the brim it is difficult to apply a stud in between two studs that are already on the hat. Work from left to right to apply the studs consecutively.

7 | Continue to Apply Studs

After you have attached each stud, take the time to make sure that it is straight and in line with the other studs. Crooked studs can go unnoticed until you have applied more studs that don't fit together quite right.

EMBELLISHMENTS | Appliqué and Buttons

TUTORIAL

Appliqué and Buttons

Appliqué is a kind of decorative patching that allows you to cut your own fabric shapes and attach them to clothing. Buttons can be as decorative or as functional as you please. Both are a great way to turn any plain article of clothing into a folksy treat.

What You'll Need:

- Buttons
- Scrap fabric
- Felt in various colors
- Iron-on interfacing
- Embroidery thread
- Scissors
- Chalk
- Measuring tape
- Embroidery needle
- Freezer paper
- Sewing needle
- Straight pins
- Thread
- Buttonhole thread

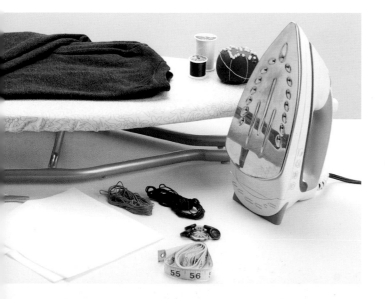

Get Prepared:

This retired purple sweater is in need of a nip and tuck, so in this tutorial we will learn how to add both functional and decorative buttons. Then we will sew on two different kinds of appliqués to create a design.

Colored felt can be bought in sheets or by the yard. Choose a thin knit sweater that will be easy to manage when it is cut up the middle. Once you have the hang of this technique, it will be easier to move on to thick sweaters and lacy shawls. For more embroidery stitches, see page 158.

1 | Chalk the Middle and Buttonholes

Use your measuring tape to measure across the front of the garment. Find the middle and mark with the chalk. Move up the garment, measuring and marking with the chalk until you have a vertical chalk line that divides the garment in half. Measure this line and divide it by how many buttons you would like. I wanted five buttons, so I divided the middle line by five and marked my sweater accordingly.

2 | Cut the Garment

Cut up the middle of the garment, being careful not to stray from the chalk line.

3 | Add Interfacing

Cut a ½in (1cm) wide piece of interfacing as long as the middle of the garment. Set your iron to the highest non-steam setting. Iron the interfacing to each inside edge of the front of the garment.

4 | Hem the Edges

We will need to fold in the new edges of the garment and stitch them to give a finished look. Fold the edge in about ½in (1cm), pinning with straight pins as you go. Dog-ear the upper edge of the fold. Thread your sewing needle with a thread that matches the color of the garment. Sew a straight-stitch all the way down the front of the garment, staying about ⅛in (3mm) from the jagged edge of your cut.

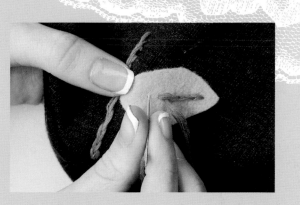

5 | Making Buttonholes

To mark the buttonholes, first chalk a vertical line that is a little shorter than the length of your button, and at least ¼in (5mm) from the edge of the garment. Cut along this small line. Test the hole by sliding a button through. It should fit snugly, but you should not have to work hard to get it through. For our buttonholes, we are going to use buttonhole thread, which is thicker than regular sewing thread. You can use a buttonhole thread to match the garment, or try something in a contrasting color to play up the buttonholes.

To start sewing the buttonhole, insert the needle in the middle of the buttonhole, in between the two layers of fabric. That way, your knot will end up in between these two layers of fabric. Pull the thread through. You should have thread hanging from the middle of the buttonhole. Now, insert the needle through the buttonhole and into the wrong side of the fabric, and out through the right side of the fabric so that it comes out next to where it came out the first time.

A buttonhole stitch allows the thread to loop under the needle to create a small knot. To do this, insert the needle into the fabric, making sure that the thread loops under the needle, as shown. Pull the needle through. Make close stitches all the way around the buttonhole.

6 | Cut and Attach Felt Appliqués

Cut shapes from the felt pieces and lay them in place on the garment. Next, we are going to use the embroidery thread to create a split stitch. To make this stitch, insert your needle into the back of the garment and through the middle of the felt shape. Complete a small straight-stitch, poking the needle back through the felt and fabric. Push the needle back up to make it go right through the middle of your last stitch, effectively splitting the stitch, as shown (alternately, you can use the similar chain stitch, as shown on page 159).

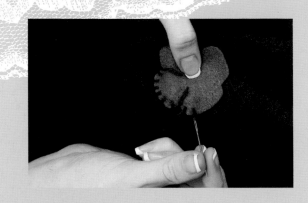

7 | Whipstitch the Felt Appliqué Edges

We will use a whipstitch to secure the edges of the felt shapes to the garment. Insert the needle at the top of the shape, then exit through the garment fabric only, just off the edge of the felt shape. Insert the needle

again, this time on the felt shape. Exit again just off of the felt, then enter again on the felt. Repeat all the way around the felt shape, then knot and clip your thread.

8 | Create a Fabric Appliqué

To create an appliqué with fabric, you will need to choose a shape, then cut a piece of fabric that is 1/4in (5mm) larger than the finished design. Iron a piece of freezer paper to the back of the fabric. This will make it easier to stitch onto the garment.

Stitch the fabric shape to the sweater, folding in the raw edge of the fabric as you go. Use small stitches and sew close to the folded edge. This way, the raw edges are trapped inside and will not unravel. Once the appliqué is mostly stitched, use tweezers to pull the freezer paper out before completing the final stitches.

9 | Sew on the Buttons

In this project, we have a couple of different buttons. Most of the buttons that close the cardigan are shank buttons, and the buttons on the flower and collar are flat buttons.

To sew on a flat button, insert the needle into the back of the fabric and straight-stitch twice to anchor the thread. Lay a straight pin across the top of the button. This will act as a spacer so that there will be room for the buttonhole fabric to lie under the button. Note that decorative buttons like the one on the flower will not need a spacer. Pull the needle through a hole in the button, then down through the opposite hole in the button, with the thread overlapping the straight pin. On a four-hole button, repeat with the other two holes. Tie and clip the thread on the inside of the garment. Slip the spacer pin out.

To sew on a shank button, insert the needle through the back of the cardigan and stitch a couple of times to anchor the thread. Place the button over this stitching. Use a whipstitch to sew the button to the garment, moving out of the fabric, through the shank, and into the fabric again. Five or six stitches will work well to hold your shank button in place. Knot and snip the thread on the inside of the garment.

Toys and Trinkets

Charms and small toys can add instant personality to whatever they are attached to. Assembled on clothing, they can create a hint of sparkly nostalgia or just a playful theme.

What You'll Need:

- An old pocket watch
- Large chain or metal belt
- Small gears
- Brooch settings
- Decorative jewelry findings
- Stud earrings
- Jump-rings
- Pins and brooches
- Large clasps
- Broken watch faces
- Pliers
- Large needle
- Buttonhole thread
- Scissors
- Hot glue
- Felt

Get Prepared:

Most of the elements here are from the bottom of my jewelry box. I found the small gears in the scrapbooking section of my local craft store. Try easy-to-find trinkets like keys, pendants, rings, or even small toys. An important part of collecting your elements is keeping a theme in mind. Too many random charms will simply look like a bunch of stuff attached to your purse. Decide on a theme and stick with it. I chose a steampunk style for this leather purse.

1 | Hot-Glue Elements Together

For the centerpiece of my bag, I wanted to add gears and a busted watch to a butterfly brooch setting. To do this, I added a dot of hot glue to the setting and pressed on my findings.

2 | Add Jump-Rings to Trinkets

Use pliers to attach jump-rings to available points, like the wings on this brooch setting. Jump-rings are useful because they can be attached to chains or even D-rings that are often found on purses.

3 | Replace the Strap with a Chain

I am going to replace the boring leather strap on my bag with a ringed metal belt. You can use large lobster clasps or jump-rings to attach a chain or belt to the purse. It will be easy to hook these clasps onto the metal D-rings of this purse.

4 | Sew on Trinkets

Thread a needle with at least 6in (15cm) of buttonhole thread. Whipstitch the gears, brooch settings, and other findings to your piece. If you're accessorizing a leather piece, use a large needle and avoid sewing through two layers of leather.

5 | **Attaching Smooth Trinkets**
Some of your treasures may not have convenient holes in the design. These can't be sewn on alone, but you can add felt to create a stitchable backing. Cut a piece of felt to the size of your trinket. Hot-glue the

felt onto the back of the trinket, using just a few points of glue. Too much glue will make it difficult to sew through the felt. Stitch the felt backing to the purse, then trim any backing that shows from the front.

6 | **Placing Studs**
Use stud earrings to hold in some of the elements of your design, and add a little bling. Pierce flat trinkets with holes in them, like this watch face.

Add the back to the earring on the inside of the piece. Hot-glue the earring back, clip the extra stud length, then add another drop of hot glue to the top. This will keep the stud from coming loose and also prevent it scraping against your skin.

7 | Add Earrings and Pins
Just as we added studs to stick items to the piece, you can also add dangling earrings and pins to the design.

Trim

At the edges of every garment lives a trim or hem. Folded hems are used to create a finished look and preserve the raw edges of fabric. Trim is also useful in this aspect, but generally has more decorative purposes. Fringe, eyelet, and piping are great examples of trims that can alter the entire attitude of a garment.

114

What You'll Need:

- Knit or cotton garment
- Lace
- Fusible interfacing
- Needle
- Thread
- Straight pins
- Measuring tape
- Chalk
- Scissors
- Iron
- Ironing board
- Sewing machine (optional)

Get Prepared:

Most trim is simply straight-stitched along a hem or tucked in-between seams. We are going to try something a little different by turning lace fabric into a trim that permeates the structure of a skirt.

To bring the look together, use a thread on the bottom of the lace that matches your garment. The garment will need to be a knit or cotton material—thin satin and silk garments do not take kindly to being clipped and stitched along the bottom.

1 | Sketch the Design
Use chalk to draw freehand the new edge of your garment. You can try a drip pattern like ours, but zigzags, jutting rectangles, and curves are also great options. Remember to only go as detailed as you are willing to deal with later. This is a great way to shorten a skirt that is too long, but keep in mind that the missing portion of the skirt will be replaced with lace, so don't go too high.

2 | Cut the Lace
Decide how much lace you would like to replace the bottom of the piece. Measure from the highest point of your chalked design down to the hem. Do you want to lengthen the garment with extra lace or keep it around the same length? For our design we needed an 8in (20cm) tall strip of lace to back our curvy design and create more curves along the bottom. Measure the width of the hem and multiply this by two. Add 2in (5cm) for a seam allowance. This number is the length of lace you will need to trim the bottom.

3 | Iron on the Interfacing
Interfacing will help to keep the cut fabric manageable while we sew, and will work to strengthen the hem through normal wear and tear. Iron on a sheet of interfacing that is tall enough to cover all of your chalked design.

4 | Cut the Hem
Cut along the chalked design. Be very careful not to fold the fabric as you snip, and work slowly around curves. Taking your time here will pay off later.

5 | Straight-Stitch and Satin-Stitch the Hem

Pin the lace to the inside of the garment. Make sure that the top of the lace is overlapping the cut lines on your garment by at least ¹⁄₂in (1cm). Double-check this, because once you stop sewing, it will be very frustrating to find out that the lace has not been positioned high enough to back every part of the design.

Straight-stitch along all of the curves of the garment, working about ¹⁄₈in (3mm) away from the edge. This should be a "basting" stitch, which means long stitches that are meant to hold the lace temporarily in place rather than permanently stitching it on.

Once the basting stitches are in place, we will satin-stitch the edges of the hem to the lace (see page 159). Place the stitches very close together. If working on a sewing machine, set the machine to a tight zigzag stitch.

6 | For Skirts with Slits

If you have a skirt with a slit in it, as shown, then you can start your straight-stitching down the length of the slit. Move on to stitch the lace along the curves.

7 | Trim and Satin-Stitch the Lace

Now that the lace is attached to the skirt, take a look at your design. Do you want to cut the bottom of the lace to match the design on the garment? The bottom of our lace is a close imitation of the waves on the skirt. Cut the lace to shape it according to your taste. Satin-stitch all along the bottom of the lace, just as we did with the skirt. When finished, hide the hanging thread by weaving it back through the last few stitches.

Patricia Valery

Patricia Valery is an independent fashion designer from Florida. Her clothing is always made from cruelty-free materials. She handles every aspect of the design process, from pattern creation to final sewing.

patriciavalery.com

When did you start embellishing and designing your own clothing?

I started sewing and designing when I was around 12 years old. I spent much of my youth living in South America. Down there it's customary to pass skills down through the generations. There was a year when my parents went on a business trip for a month and left me with my grandmother, who had a sewing business. She showed me the basics and I fell in love with sewing. Since she made her living off her craft, my grandmother stressed attention to detail on the basics, more than knowing a wide breadth of techniques.

How do you decide to add certain fabric flowers, ribbon, or trim to a particular piece?

I always start with an inspiration board and I usually have a vague idea of what I want to do, but I don't sketch much, and I allow a lot of freedom during the process. Because I am an independent designer my biggest limitations are money and materials. Many times I don't find what I'm looking for and I have to improvise. This is really where I have to get creative. I'll often find the right fabric but not the right color, or vice versa. And because of this I have to make changes to other items in the collection so that it is cohesive.

I hand sew almost every item I sell. I also try to keep my clothing affordable for everyone, so I usually work with simple construction techniques and use embellishments to make my pieces more interesting.

What is the biggest challenge for you as a designer and seamstress?

As an independent designer my biggest limitation is money. I would love for my pieces to be more technical, but the amount of time it takes to make something like that raises the final cost. Pattern-making is really tedious as well. A simple design takes about three to four days to make. I have to pick whether I need to drape it or draft it. Once I've done this, I make a muslin sample. After the sample, I have to make small modifications and transfer them onto my original pattern. I then have to remake the dress in the intended fabric. Sometimes that fabric won't look the way I planned, so I'll have to pick a new one. Once I've finished the sample, I have to trace my pattern and grade it (upsize and downsize), which I do manually. Finally, I scan the pattern into my computer so that I have a backup in case something happens to the original paper pattern. I could probably go on for days with all of the limitations, but in the end I really love what I do and I don't mind dealing with these little things as much as I would mind working for someone else.

What advice would you give to someone who is just starting out with adding embellishments to their clothing?

Take notes! When I was in college I had a sewing instructor who would assign projects, like putting in a zipper, or making a collar. But what was most helpful was that she would make us write step-by-step instructions in our own words. We would keep the sewn samples along with the instructions in a binder. At the end of the term I had a folder with over 30 samples. This has been the most valuable item in my collection. I have a horrible time following instrutions out of a book, so writing these techniques in my own words has really helped me out. Everyone learns differently. Figure out your personal learning style and use it to your advatage—even if it requires a few extra steps.

As an independent artist, how do you keep your work in the public eye?

PatriciaValery.com is my best tool for reaching the public. I don't actually sell there, but boutique owners and bloggers can always find me through my site. I sell on Etsy and to a handful of brick-and-mortar stores around the USA. I also keep a blog, Twitter and Facebook accounts, and all that fun stuff.

Top far left: Olivia top with white trim.

Top right: Top with heart-shaped embellishment.

Right: Seersucker dress with vintage pink trim.

EMBELLISHMENTS | Gallery

Above: Beaded cape from Monsoon.

Right: Embellished bikini from River Island.

Above: Floral print skirt with pom-pom trim by Patricia Valery.

120

Above: Maxi dress with sequin details by Monsoon.

Left: Besace Costa bag with leather appliqué and trim by Antik Batik.

Above: Chiffon dress with embellished waistband by Patricia Valery.

EMBELLISHMENTS | Gallery

Right: Appliquéd tote bag from Accessorize.

Below: Hairband with feather and brooch embellishments from Accessorize.

LOVELY

Above: Tank top with sequin design by Lipsy.

Above: Beaded sandals by French Connection.

Above: Vintage studded beret from Beyond Retro.

Left: Scarf with beads and sequins from Monsoon.

Above: Dress embellished with beads and sequins from Monsoon.

Above: Clutch purse with feather and brooch embellishments by Angee W.

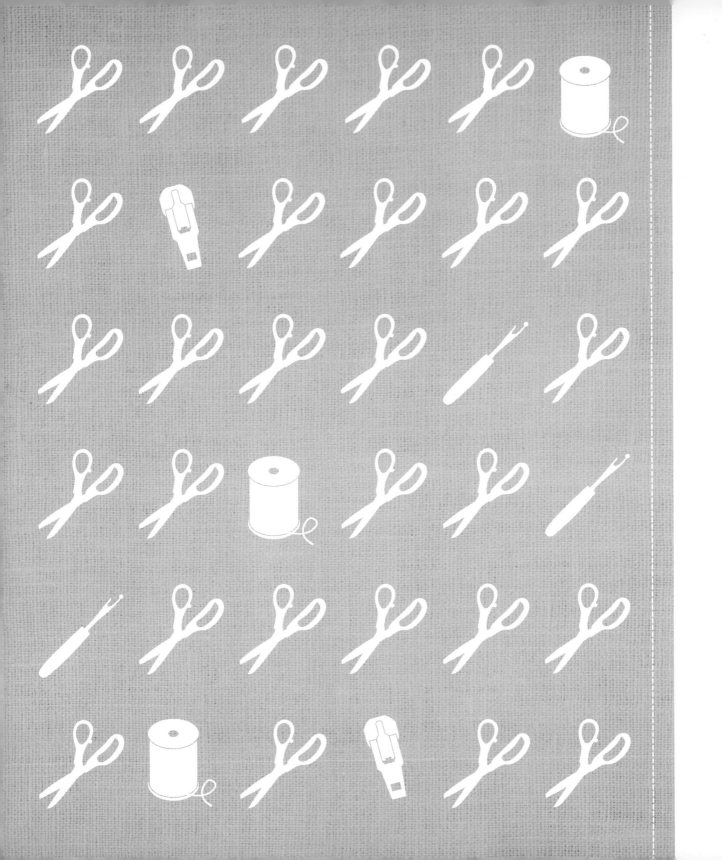

Chapter 6

DECONSTRUCTION

"Somehow I saved $20. With it I bought an elegant leather coat. Patent leather, shiny and lovely. But suddenly I saw that it looked too new. How were people to know that I was a flyer if I wore a coat that was too new? Wrinkles! That was it. There just had to be wrinkles. So—I slept in it for three nights."

— Amelia Earhart

Distressed, cut, and restitched clothing has the appeal of being loved, appreciated—and then hacked to pieces. Methodically destroying our clothes may seem counterproductive to a love of fashion, but in reality these clothes have been given a good deal more attention than something new off the rack.

One of the questions I am most often asked as a designer is why wrecked threads are so coveted. They look terrible, so why try so hard to get the look? Clothes that have been scraped, picked, and even sandblasted are symbols of time and experience—time spent working, playing, and simply living an individual life inside of our clothes. The potential for past romps, bygone relationships, and hidden knowledge add an instant intrigue to any weathered garment. Just as wrinkles on our faces describe years of experience, so do the wrinkles on Amelia Earhart's jacket.

Another side to deconstruction is the possibility of upcycled style. When our over-loved garments have been worn or stained beyond repair, they can be reassembled into all-new fashions. Slice off the legs of jeans and you have a cute pair of country shorts. Cut squares from an old t-shirt to create a brand new tote bag. Once you know how to cut and stitch, a closet full of ill-fitting or tattered clothes is just as good as a trip to the fabric store.

DECONSTRUCTION

TUTORIAL

Distressed

A destroyed look on your clothes can give the impression that you've been around the block. This isn't your first rodeo. You weren't born yesterday. I mean, look at these rips … you must know something about the ways of the world. Well, they look cool, anyway.

What You'll Need:

- Denim jeans/bag
- Scissors
- Seam ripper

Get Prepared:

Somewhere out there, someone is paying lots of money—right now—for a designer pair of worn-out jeans. I'll show you how to mess up your own jeans at home using everyday household items. You can go for the naturally worn look, or just shred them to pieces.

Denim jeans most often have a weave of blue-and-white threads. The blue threads run vertically from the top to the bottom of the fabric. The white threads run horizontally across the front of the fabric. These are the threads you see strung across holes on shredded jeans. The following method of picking the blue threads will leave a crop of white threads intact to complete the shredded look.

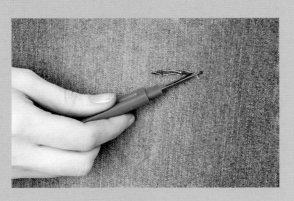

1 | **Tear Jeans with a Seam Ripper**
Choose where you would like to add a shredded effect to your jeans. The fronts of the thigh, knees, and near the hemline are popular choices. Insert the point of the seam ripper and move it across the fabric to cut a small 2in (5cm) opening. It is important to try to cut as horizontally as possible so that you do not destroy the white threads.

2 | **Pull the Threads from the Weave**
Use the tip of the seam ripper to catch the white threads from the edges of your cut. Gently pull these white threads from the vertical blue threads, moving them toward the center of the hole.

3 | **Widen the Gaps**
To adjust the width of the shredded area, you can use the seam ripper to catch blue threads on the edges of your torn hole. Slice them individually with the seam ripper to widen the gap. Attempting to cut these edges with scissors could cause you to accidentally cut the white threads and ruin the strung-out look you are trying to achieve.

4 | **Create Columns of Weave Between the Gaps**
As you widen the shredded area, you may notice that the holey areas may be too saggy or loose. Try clustering shredded holes together to give the look of one distressed area. This will leave columns of the blue-and-white weave intact, allowing for shorter exposed white threads and retaining the strength of the jeans. To do this, pick out a 2in (5cm) wide area of shred. Skip ¼in (5mm) of fabric and start a new hole with the seam ripper. Be careful not to pick away the ¼in (5mm) area you have left intact.

128

5 | Clip Extra Fringe

As you work, the blue threads will start to feather out and hang down from the shredded holes. Clip this fringe close to the fabric or leave it to hang as fringe.

6 | Pick at Pocket Edges

To distress the side and back pockets of the jeans, pick away at the blue threads along the tops of the pockets. Like the legs of the jeans, this will leave strips of white threads behind.

7 | Pick at the Hem

Pick the bottom hem of the pants, this time leaving the blue threads to hang as fringe. For more distressed effects, try using spray bleach, as seen on page 24.

 DECONSTRUCTION

Cut and Slashed

Fringed, bleached, and paint-splattered, damaged garments hint at a mysterious incident endured by the wearer. While they may appear accidental, these grunge looks often involve more work than meets the eye.

What You'll Need:

- Jersey knit garment
- Scissors
- Seam Ripper

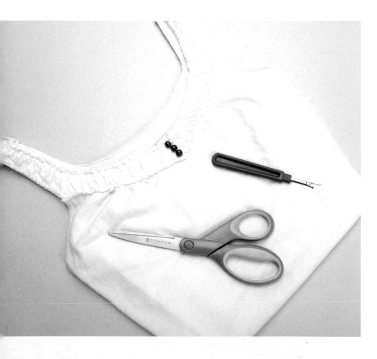

Get Prepared:

A few hours of careful picking and pulling are required to create the look of unearthly claws. I'll show you how to loosen the knit on any jersey garment to make this bold look.

You will need a jersey knit garment for this technique. This is important because we are actually unraveling the knit to create the horizontal lines of thread.

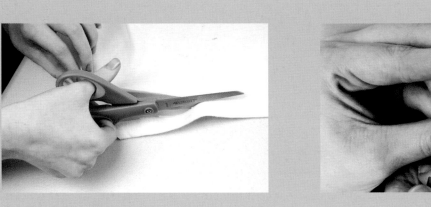

1 | **Remove the Shirt Hem**
Cut off the shirt hem just above the stitching.

2 | **Start the Shredded Area**
Pick at the edge of the fabric so that the knit begins to unravel. The little "V" shapes of the knit will come loose, leaving only horizontal threads. Loosen up ½in (1cm) of knit fabric across the bottom of the garment.

3 | **Start Popping the Knit**
Pinch the first few threads and pull. This will start a "ladder" pattern of threads popping loose from the knit as shown. As you pull at the ladder of thread, the knit can sometimes catch and prevent the threads from coming loose. When this happens, just use the tip of the seam ripper to coax the thread into action.

4 | **Pull the Knit Up the Shirt**
Continue to pull and pick at the threads, moving all the way to the top of the garment. You can widen the shredded line by working more columns of knit from the bottom.

5 | **Add Rips in the Pattern**
Clip some of the horizontal threads to create gaps in the design. These gaps can also be made in the middle of the garment to create new shredded areas without starting at the hem line.

6 | **Push Stitches Toward the Middle**
To get a lot of tiny lines running through your shredded work, push some of the vertical seams toward the middle of the shredded areas. Use the tip of the seam ripper to gently push out the vertical threads.

DECONSTRUCTION

Darning

(TUTORIAL)

Back in the olden days, people took their sweet time to knit socks and sweaters. When these inevitably grew holes, it was a no-brainer to darn them shut. Darning is a way to weave closed those pesky tears with yarn.

What You'll Need:

- Garment in need of repair
- Yarn
- Darning needle
- Scissors
- Chalk

132

Get Prepared:

Use a yarn weight that is thin enough to match the look of the garment. If your yarn on hand is too thick, just clip a portion and separate some of the threads before you begin.

However, instead of using black yarn to darn shut a hole in the sleeve of this sweater, I'm going to go whole-hog with decoy designs working in bright, contrasting yarns.

1 | **Chalk Out the Designs**
We are going to create a lot of decorative darning on this piece to distract from the stitched hole. To start, chalk out simple shapes around the garment.

2 | **Create a Running Stitch**
Darning is all about weaving horizontal and vertical sets of running stitches. We are going to begin by creating the entire set of vertical stitches. Begin a running stitch by inserting the long darning needle into the fabric. You do not need to start on the inside of the garment; the tail-end of the yarn can be woven in later. Move the needle in and out of the fabric, catching the fabric onto the needle in intervals as shown. Pull the needle through, creating a set of stitching in one fluid movement. Continue to work each row of the design until you have finished all of the stitches in one direction.

3 | **Weave Across the Stitches**
Once the vertical stitches are all in, we can work on the horizontal stitches that will cross them. Just as before, work the needle in and out of the fabric, then pull the yarn through all of the stitches at once. This time, you will be weaving under the vertical stitches whenever they cross the needle.

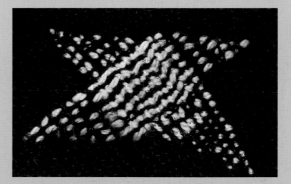

4 | **Decorative Darning**
This finished bit of decorative darning shows the effect of weaving two different colors of yarn. Once you get used to creating running stitches, it is easy to expand your work to include more colors and varied stitch sizes.

5 | **Push Stitches Toward the Middle**
The whole reason we have darned this sweater is to repair a little hole on the sleeve. This is done in the same way as decorative darning, except that the running stitches will cross over the gap in the fabric. You will weave the horizontal and vertical stitches in the same way as decorative darning, except that the yarn will create a new fabric at the middle of the design, as shown.

Zippers

Stuck, broken, off-track, and toothy; zippers are the busiest parts of our wardrobe. No wonder they are also the first to break down.

What You'll Need:

- **Zippers**
- **Scissors**
- **Straight pin**
- **Needle**
- **Embroidery thread**

Get Prepared:

When a zipper needs to be replaced, you can actually reuse it to create a bouquet of upcycled style. Here I'll show you how to roll and stitch zippers into studded roses that will last longer than their previous jacket-zipping lives.

Zippers can be harvested off of old jackets, but they can also be inexpensive to purchase if you are looking for a particular color. I've made a headband as thin plastic and fabric headbands are the easiest to stitch to, but you could also use this technique to embellish a jacket lapel or bag.

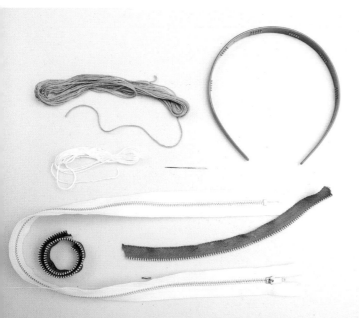

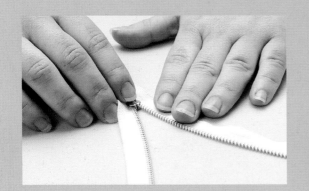

1 | Harvest the Zipper

To get the entire zipper from a jacket, use a seam ripper to remove the stitches that hold it in place. Whether you use a new or used zipper, you will need to cut away the stoppers at each end. This is easy if you cut at an angle between the teeth. Slide the zipper head off and set it aside.

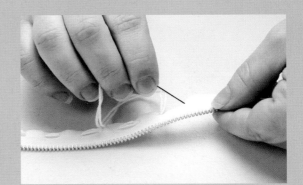

2 | Baste and Gather the Zipper

Thread a large needle with embroidery thread. This thread is thick and sturdy enough to hold the zipper together. Fold over and stitch the end of the zipper. Make long, loose straight stitches across the zipper for a few inches. Pull on the thread so that the zipper begins to curl in on itself.

3 | Stitch and Pull Again

Continue to stitch a few inches, then pull the string. As you work, the rose shape will begin to form as the zipper curls up.

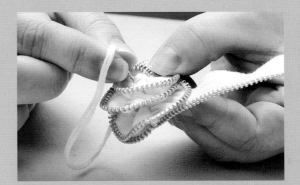

4 | Stitch Together

Once the entire zipper is stitched, carefully curl it so that the spiraling teeth lay in layers to form the rose. Insert the needle into the middle of the flower, stitching together the layers. Stitch here and there, catching the fabric on the zipper where needed to keep the layers together.

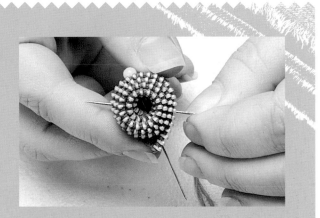

5 | **Add the Zipper Head**
Place the zipper head at the center of the rose and whipstitch it onto the zipper fabric.

6 | **Rosebud Roll**
Roll up a small zipper and use a straight pin to hold it in place. Stitch the rosebud together near the bottom with a matching embroidery thread, sewing through it in a cross pattern so that it is secured in both directions.

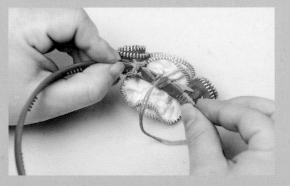

7 | **Stitch to the Headband**
On the inside of most headbands you will find patches of small bumps that help the headband grab onto hair. This is also a great spot to catch thread. Whipstitch the bottoms of the flowers to these areas of the headband. See page 146 for the finished piece.

DECONSTRUCTION

TUTORIAL Stitch

There are a lot of utilitarian sewing stitches, each with its own purpose. While some are used for holding seams together, others prevent fabric from unraveling or strengthen a garment. When you know a few basic stitches, you are ready to repair or upcycle your wardrobe.

What You'll Need:

- **Needle**
- **Thread**
- **Scissors**
- **Chalk**

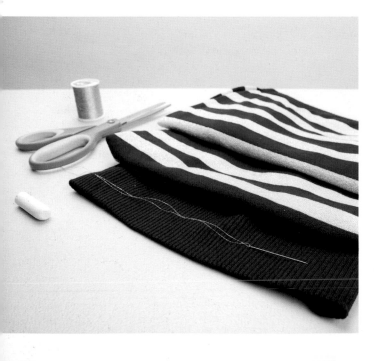

Get Prepared:

In this tutorial, you will learn a lot of useful stitches that will come in handy for all your sewing projects. I am using a contrasting color of thread in order to make our work more visible. Unless you are going for a funky look, you will want to use matching thread on all of your seams. I'm upcycling a sweater with stretchy ribbing at the bottom, but you can omit this part and simply hem the edges of any sweater without adding trim.

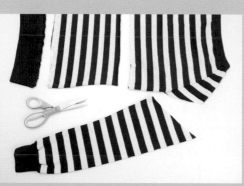

1 | **Chop It Up**
To upcycle this sweater into a wrap, we will need to remove the sleeves, the lower half of the sweater, and the stretchy hem. Get in front of a mirror and decide how long you want your trimmed sleeves. Mark your new sleeve length with chalk, keeping in mind that you will be adding the elastic hem of the sweater to the sleeve cuffs. Mark just below the bust line to determine where the sweater will be chopped in half. Cut at your marks, and just above the stitching that holds the stretchy hem onto the sweater.

2 | **Cut Down the Middle**
Cut from the collar all the way down the sweater. You can cut rounded edges at the bottom, or leave them straight. For this sweater, we trimmed curved edges.

3 | **Stitch the Front**
Fold the front edges of the wrap inward. Straight-stitch ¼in (5mm) from the edge (see the following photo of the straight stitch) to create a smooth hem all the way down the front of the wrap.

4 | Prepare the Ribbing

We had enough ribbing on this sweater to add it to the bottom hem of the wrap and sleeves. I loosely wrapped the ribbing around one sleeve to measure out how much would be needed to trim it. Remember to allow about 1in (2.5cm) for the seams. Cut two of these lengths, one for each sleeve.

The remaining length of ribbing can be used to hem the bottom edge of the wrap. Mine was just enough to wrap around the back and a bit up the front. Experiment with the available ribbing. You could gather it to create ruffled edges on the front of the wrap, skip the sleeves for more ribbing all the way around the bottom hem, or use no trim at all.

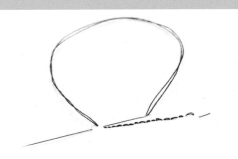

5 | Straight-Stitch the Seam

Start at the middle of the back of the wrap. Place the ribbing on top of the edge of the wrap, right sides together. Straight-stitch the ribbing to the wrap, working about ½in (1cm) from the edge. To straight-stitch, insert the needle into the fabric, then out again as shown in this example. The ½in (1cm) of fabric left at the edge is called the "seam allowance," and is important for keeping the fabric together.

6 | Backstitch the Seam

A backstitch is used to strengthen seams that will endure a lot of wear. To backstitch, bring the needle up through the fabric, then back into the fabric just behind where the needle emerged, and up again just in front of the thread, as shown in this example. Repeat for a hearty stitch that can take a lot of abuse.

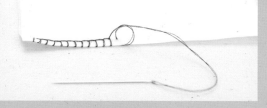

7 | Blanket-Stitch the Seam Allowance

To prevent our wrap from coming unraveled, we need to blanket-stitch the edges of the seam allowance. This will prevent the tiny threads from coming loose during wear and washing. Insert the needle into the fabric at the edge of the seam allowance. Loop over the edge of the fabric, then insert the needle again. Guide the needle through the loop of thread as it exits the fabric, as shown in this example. While blanket stitch is great for preserving the seam allowance, it is also a great decorative stitch that can be used down the front of a garment.

8 | Sew on the Sleeve Trim

Place the ribbing on top of the sleeves with the right sides of the fabric together. Straight-stitch and backstitch the ribbing to the sleeve, just as with the bottom of the wrap. Start sewing at the armpit area so that the edges of the ribbing will be hidden when worn. After the ribbing is attached to the fabric, straight-stitch the two ends of the ribbing together (right sides together) to finish the tube of the sleeve.

Broken Ghost Couture

Jana Foehrenbach's first love has always been art in many different media. From the time she was old enough to hold a crayon, her passion for creating was strong. Sewing was something she had dabbled in, but it wasn't until she owned a consignment clothing shop that she began designing. Many pieces of clothing that had "no home" became her supply of fabric and she set to work creating unique, fun garments. Jana loves the "soul" behind second-hand and vintage fabrics. Being a self-taught seamstress and designer has empowered Jana to "invent" techniques of her own, resulting in some whimsical, one-of-a-kind pieces. She set up the Broken Ghost Couture label to sell her work. brokenghost.com

How did you start upcycling clothes?

A large part of society has "gone green" by some degree over the last five years. I knew there would be people who love the idea of re-using fabrics as much as I do. I have always loved items that are not brand new. If I need a table for my kitchen, for example, I will always source out a second-hand one first and that attitude carries over to almost every aspect of my life.

How do you approach an old piece of clothing and envision it as something new?

Well, I have to say, I plan nothing! My creative process starts by searching through a random pile of clothing, eyeing what could be the start of it and then searching for colors, patterns to add to it. My style of design is "make it up as I go." I find it challenging to make custom pieces because it alters this spontaneous thought process and becomes more planned.

What is the biggest challenge to upcycling? What do you do when a project goes wrong?

I sometimes make a small mistake when I'm sewing, like a pucker or crooked seam, but this quickly becomes an opportunity to add a new design element to the piece. Instead of taking it apart to start again, I change up the design by adding a ruffle, lace, or another color block to it.

What advice would you give to someone who is beginning to change up their own clothing?

When starting off with a certain garment, look at it upside down, sideways, and inside-out. Sometimes the best texture is from the wrong side of the fabric. A shirt can be turned upside down and made into a skirt, for example. I also *love* trims. Trims are great for adding interest and texture to your piece.

Jana Foehrenbach creates characterful pieces for adults and children by upcycling second-hand and vintage clothes.

As an independent artist, how do you keep your work in the public eye?

Currently, my designs are only available on Etsy. I have sold at a bricks-and-mortar shop, but because I am a one-woman show, it's difficult to make items in bulk. I tend to create two or three pieces a day, so selling online sets the perfect pace for me. I have participated in fashion shows as well.

143

Above: Distressed coat by Chris Benz.

Above: Jumpsuit with zipper detail made from recycled clothing by Katie Pray.

Upcycled clothing by Broken Ghost Couture.

Above: Distressed jeans by Rain Blanken. See page 126.

Above: Slashed blouse sleeve by Gucci.

Above: Swirl cutout dress by Katie Pray.

Above: Distressed tank top and jeans from Balmain.

Chapter 7 |

SPECIALIST TECHNIQUES

"I was never a good sewer. My mom taught me. Like, with velcro up the back, and you know. Kind of looked good from the outside, but the inside was a mess."

— Gwen Stefani

Embossing could be considered an extension of both discharge and printing techniques, while marbling just might be the distant cousin of the dye projects we experienced in the Coloring chapter ... or is it printing? Some methods of clothing customization are are not as easily categorized as the previous techniques.

This does not mean that the following projects are especially difficult to learn or execute. Methods such as leather punch and punch needle are very specific to the task, so they have been placed here as a kind of bonus material to complement the skills you have gleaned from previous chapters. The looks are specific, but definitely worth learning.

Adding interest to your wardrobe can sometimes mean taking on unexpected tasks. I found myself suspending paint onto a tray of goo one day and knew that marbling was something special beyond your everyday tie-dye project. I was trying something that not everyone has the chance to experience, and I couldn't wait to share what I'd learned. Unique methods of making your style seem unlikely, but they are just as unforgettable and often repeated.

SPECIALIST TECHNIQUES

TUTORIAL

Punch Needle

Punch needle (or needlepunch) is a way to easily embroider fabric with fluffy loops of thread. It is often used for folk art wall hangings, but can be applied to clothing as long as it is secured well with fabric glue.

What You'll Need:

- Embroidery thread
- Punch needle
- Wire threader
- Embroidery hoop
- Permanent fabric glue
- Marker
- Scissors
- Transfer paper
- Pencil
- Paper

150

Get Prepared:

You will need to separate the bulky embroidery thread into individual strands. I find that up to four or five strands together in the punch needle work well. Use fewer strands for thicker metallic threads. This is a great opportunity to cut lengths of different colors and combine them to make your own variegated thread. I used about 2ft (60cm) of embroidery thread at a time to keep the length manageable.

Be advised that punch needle is a simple but slow process; filling a space can take many hours.

1 | **Draw and Transfer Your Design**
Compose or print out an image that will fit nicely on your piece. Turn the piece inside out. Lay a sheet of transfer paper between your design and the piece. Trace the design with a pencil, pressing firmly to transfer the image onto the inside of the piece.

2 | **Thread the Shaft of the Punch Needle**
To thread the punch needle, use the thin wire threader that came with your punch needle tool. Insert the threader into the front of the punch needle and through the shaft so that it pokes out of the back of the tool. Loop about 1in (2.5cm) of the embroidery thread through the wire loop. Pull the wire through the punch-needle shaft.

3 | **Thread the Needle of the Punch Needle**
Remove the thread from the wire threader. This time, insert the threader up through the eye of the needle. Then guide the embroidery thread through the wire loop. Pull the thread through the eye of the needle. The small wire punch needle threader is easy to lose, so put it in a safe place as soon as you are done threading. I like to wrap a small piece of masking tape on the threader to make it more visible.

4 | **Start Punching**
Let about 1in (2.5cm) of the thread hang from the end of the needle before you begin. Start at the beginning of a line on your transferred design. Gently push the punch needle through the fabric until it stops.

5 | Pull Out the Needle, Scrape, and Punch

Gently lift the needle out, but do not pull it all the way off of the fabric. Lifting the needle off of the fabric will pull at the thread too much and cause the loops on the other side to come loose or look too small.

With the needle tilted at a 45-degree angle, gently scrape along the fibers of the fabric, skipping a couple of threads in the weave to your next punching spot. This scraping motion will prevent the thread from pulling out of the other side of the piece, and also helps you to count how many threads in the fabric weave you have skipped over. Space your punches about two threads at a time for a nice loopy fill on the right side of the fabric.

6 | Continue Punching

Follow a work pattern of punching, lifting, and scraping. It will be awkward at first, but soon you will get the hang of how to handle the punch needle. Periodically check the right side of the fabric to see how you are doing on the loops. If some of the loops are too small, you can easily pull out the work you have done and punch that portion over again. When you run out of one color of thread, just make sure the ends of the thread are poking out of the wrong side of the fabric, then reload the needle and begin again.

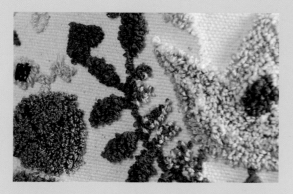

7 | Create Lines and Fills

For lines, start at the beginning of a line and work your way all the way to the end. For filling large spaces, try working from the edges to the middle. Experiment with fills—add more space between punches for a lacy look, or fit them close together for a thick carpet of color. If you have plotted a large design, get comfortable on the couch and prepare to put the work down before it is done. You are filling in each and every stitch, so try to imagine how long the punch needle embroidery will take to complete. This bag took over 40 hours to complete, but each stitch was just as easy as the last—it just took time. Try mixing punch needle with embroidery stitches (see page 158) for a finished look. I added a zigzag pattern at the bottom of this bag, as seen in Mexican embroidery designs.

8 | Glue the Stitches

Punch needle embroidery is usually applied to decorative wall hangings. Since we are working with a piece of clothing, you will need to apply permanent fabric glue on the back of the stitches to keep them from pulling out. This is very important because your work can be easily pulled away from the fabric by accident or during a wash cycle. Blot the applied glue to make sure that it settles into the stitches, and let it dry according to the manufacturer's directions.

Marbling

TUTORIAL

Intricate patterned swirls can be achieved on cloth through the art of marbling. While the materials we use are quite modern, this art dates back hundreds of years, and it is most popularly believed to have originated in Turkey.

154

What You'll Need:

- Acrylic paint
- Marbo Gum
- Alum
- Distilled water
- Shallow tub or tray
- Wooden skewers
- Paper towel tube
- Paper cups
- Rubber gloves

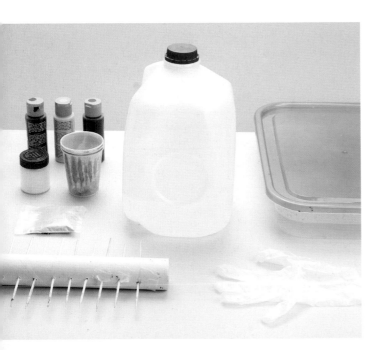

Get Prepared:

While marbling is usually used on sheets of paper and lengths of fabric, it can also be used on small accessories. I'm going to dip a pair of canvas shoes to give them a yummy, sundae finish. If you decide to use shoes for your marbling project, remove the shoelaces and treat the shoes in a bath of alum. Soak for 20 minutes in a bath of $2^1/_2$ tsp alum per quart (liter) of distilled water. Allow them to dry completely in the dryer, or air dry. Fabrics that marble well include plant-based fibers and silks.

1 | Mix the Size

In marbling, paint is floated on the surface of the "size," a slightly thick substance set in a shallow tray. I am using Marbo Gum for my size, which is easier to mix than carrageenan, a type of seaweed used in traditional marbling. There are a couple of other products available to create the size. Whatever you use, make sure to mix it exactly as directed by the manufacturer. Allow the size to set for 24 hours for the best results.

2 | Prepare the Paint

Acrylic paint will need to be watered down in order to float on the size. I put a drop of paint in paper cups, then added drops of distilled water to dilute it. I find that a "milkshake" texture works for inexpensive acrylic paint, but you should try your hand at dripping paint and adjust the mixture as needed. Different colors of paint may need different amounts of water, so don't be surprised if your recipes vary.

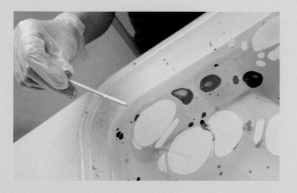

3 | Drip the Paint onto the Size

Use a skewer to drip the paint onto the size. If the paint sinks to the bottom of the tray, then it is too thick and will need a bit more water. If the paint spreads very quickly over most of the size, then it is too thin.

Drip the paint all over the surface of the size, keeping in mind that the colors dripped first will appear on top of the subsequent colors on the dyed piece.

4 | Rake the Size

If you want some fun spots on your piece, dip it in the paint dripped onto the size. For swirls and feathery patterns, you will first need to rake the size. Use a homemade rake like the one I made with a paper towel tube and wooden skewers, or freehand a design by swirling smaller tools across the surface.

For the design we made, the homemade rake was pulled vertically across the size, then horizontally, and vertically again.

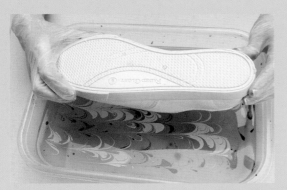

5 | Dip the Piece

Position the piece directly above the size. Slowly dip it in, then carefully rotate it to the left and right, making sure that all of the surface is saturated. Lift the piece straight out of the size.

6 | Repeat

As before, position the piece directly above the size. Slowly dip it in, then carefully rotate it to the left and right, making sure that all of the surface is saturated. Lift it straight out of the size.

SPECIALIST TECHNIQUES

TUTORIAL

Embroidery

Decorative stitches are an easy way to
personalize fabric, from handmade quilts to
machine-embroidered sportswear. While
embroidery takes time to learn and apply, the
stitches often last the life of the garment.

158

What You'll Need:

- Embroidery hoop
- Embroidery thread
- Needle
- Scissors
- Chalk

Get Prepared:

Choose a material that will be easy to stitch through, but not
too thin to hold the weight of the embroidery thread. My design
here uses five different embroidery stitches, each of which helps
to build the thickness and effects of the line art.

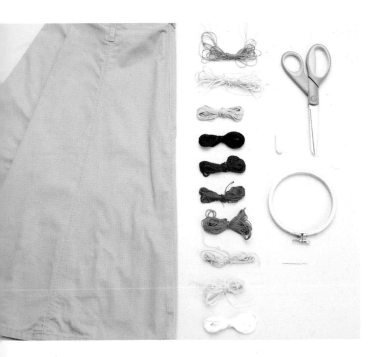

1 | **Chalk the Design**
Use chalk to sketch out the design. You can also use transfer paper if you have a print or drawn design that you would like to transfer to the fabric.

2 | **Chain Stitch**
Chain stitches are great for building lines. Bring the needle up through the fabric, and then back down into the hole, leaving a small loop of thread. Bring the needle up through the loop. Make another small loop, driving the needle back into the fabric where it emerged. Repeat.

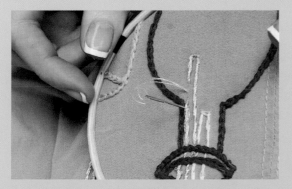

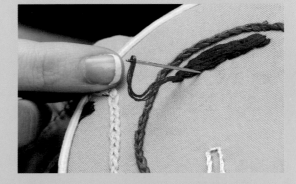

3 | **Stem Stitch**
A stem stitch is a decorative way to create long, thin lines and stems. Stitch once to begin. Bring the needle back up through the fabric to the left of where the needle was inserted.

4 | **Satin-stitch**
A satin stitch is used to fill a large area with color. Bring the needle up through the fabric at one edge of the design, cross the area to be filled, and then insert the needle. Repeat. For larger areas, use satin-stitch in short bursts to fill the space.

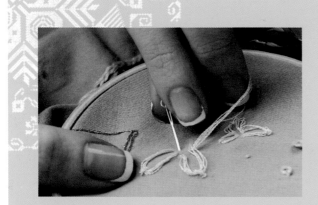

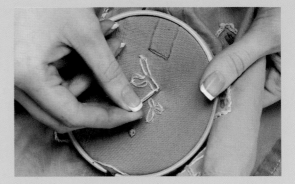

5 | Lazy Daisy
The lazy daisy stitch is used to create cute flowering designs. Pull the thread up through the fabric. Create a curve of thread and insert the needle close to where the thread emerged.

Bring the needle up at the apex of the curve of thread. Insert the needle just over the other side of the thread, pinning the curve to the fabric.

6 | French Knot
A French knot is useful for creating dots and bubbles. Pull the needle up through the fabric. Wrap the embroidery thread twice around the needle, starting at the bottom.

Insert the needle close to where the thread emerged. Pull the thread through the twists on the needle, creating a little tuft or a knot.

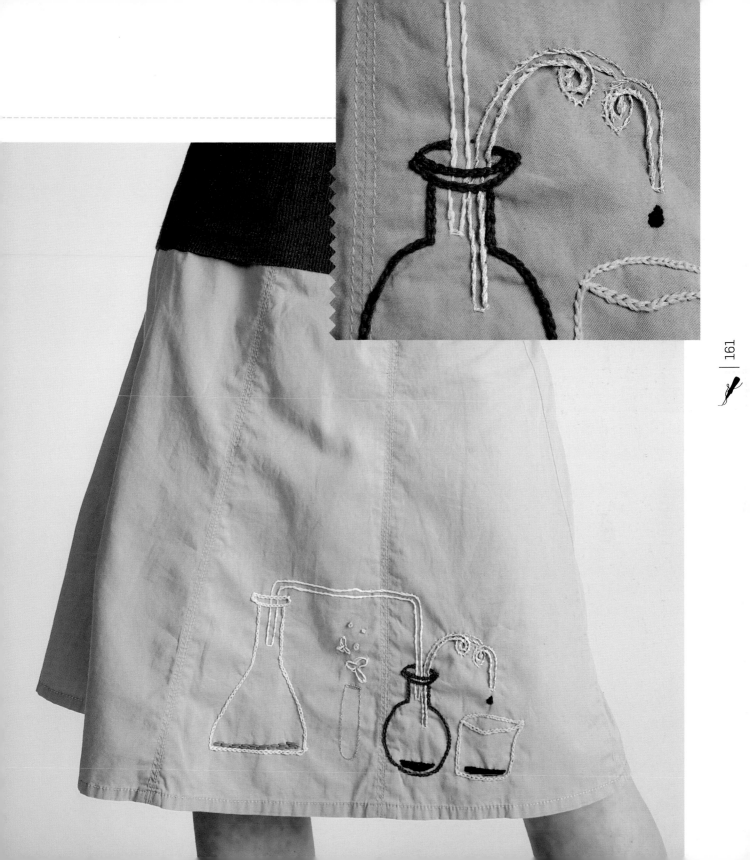

(TUTORIAL)

Embossing

Plush velvet is a fabric that can create both a luxurious and comfortable look. With the addition of gleaming embossed designs, velvet can gain an interesting sense of theme, movement, and texture.

162

What You'll Need:

- • Velvet garment
- • Rubber stamp
- • Spray bottle
- • Water
- • Iron
- • Ironing board

Get Prepared:

Hot metal has been used for centuries to impress designs on velvet, but I think we should go a simpler route for embossing at home. The only hot metal in this tutorial is an iron placed atop a rubber stamp.

Velvet can be made with varying fibers. A 60/40 acetate and rayon blend will create the best impressions, but 100% rayon and silk can also be used with good results. Synthetic materials such as nylon, acrylic, and polyester should never be used, as these have low melting points and can burn or even create noxious fumes when ironed. When you are finished, your garment will be dry-clean only.

1 | **Mist the Stamp with Water**
Spray the face of the stamp with water, enough to wet the surface. Tap the edge of the stamp against a table to shed any large drops.

2 | **Mist the Back of the Fabric**
Lay the fabric face down on the stamp, exactly where you would like your embossed image. Consider how much space you would like between stamps as you work. Spritz the back of the fabric over the stamp. It should be saturated, but not soaked.

3 | **Adjust the Iron for Pressing**
Set the iron to the highest steam setting. If you smell a funky burning while you are working, the iron is set too high for the fabric. Lower the setting a notch and try again. Make an effort to press the fabric with an area of the iron that does not have a steam hole, as these holes will leave gaps on your design. If this is unavoidable, carefully lift and move the iron periodically to evenly press the fabric.

4 | **Press the Fabric**
Press the fabric for at least 20 seconds, or until the fabric is dry over the stamp.

5 | Reveal Your Design

Peel back the fabric to reveal your embossed design. If the design is not very crisp, try to adjust the ironing time. I have found that respritzing the fabric and ironing again can help to create crisp impressions in some types of velvet.

Dealing with Heat

The heat on the stamp can sometimes melt the glue that keeps the rubber mounted to the wood block, which can cause the rubber stamp to actually slide off of the block. To avoid this, wait 10 minutes between impressions to give the stamp a chance to cool. It can also help to have two identical stamps to switch between and expedite the process.

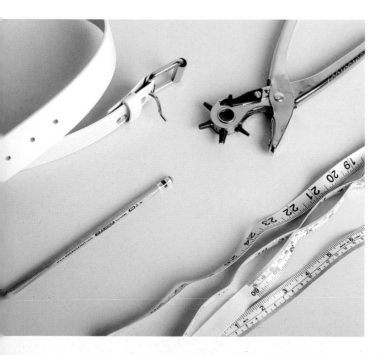

Leather Punch

TUTORIAL

Leather is a material often used in our daily wardrobe, but it can be intimidating in a customization project. Punching holes in leather is a quick and easy way to give heavy leather accessories an airy look.

What You'll Need:

- Leather belt
- Rotary leather punch
- Measuring tape
- Pencil

Get Prepared:

Leather punching is often reserved for resizing belts or assembling leather crafts. I'm going to use a rotary leather punch to make lots of different-sized holes in a plain belt, giving it a lacy design throughout.

Rotary punches can be found at most craft stores. Try picking up an old belt at the thrift store, or experiment with punching holes in used boots and leather totes.

1 | Create the Design and Mark the Holes

Use a measuring tape to determine how far you want the holes from the edges of the belt. In pencil, make a series of light marks to indicate the distance from the edge, then connect these marks to create one horizontal line down the length of the belt. I used about 1/4in (5mm) from the edge for my project. Don't press hard with the pencil; we will be erasing this line later.

Measure lengthwise along the line you just made, crossing the line in small marks to indicate the space in between holes. Continue to mark the rest of the belt, measuring horizontally and then vertically to make cross-shaped marks that will be punched. Working precisely will give your finished belt a professional look.

2 | Select the Hole Size

A rotary punch has a variety of circular punch sizes. As you plan your project, turn the wheel to switch between hole sizes, and even test the punch on scrap paper or cloth to get an idea of how big the holes will be.

3 | Punch Small Holes

Position the leather punch over one of the crosshair marks. Try to center the punch directly over the mark. Small holes are quick and easy to punch, but be careful and take your time.

4 | Punch Larger Holes

Punching large holes in leather can require some muscle power. If you are concerned about arthritis or muscle strain, stick to small decorative holes on a thin belt for your first leather-punch project (or find a burly friend to help). Erase any leftover pencil marks on your belt before wearing.

Advanced Leather Punch Kits

Punched leather doesn't have to be limited to circles. Punch hearts, stars, diamonds, and more lucky charms with specialized punch kits available online and at select craft stores. These are usually hammer punch kits, which include an assortment of hollow punches that are thwacked into the leather with a small hammer. When combining a lot of shapes, it is a good idea to carefully mark the leather with a ruler and pencil before you start to punch. Preparation of the leather is key, because once you punch, there is no going back. Remember, measure twice, punch once!

Little Dear

Aimee Ray of Little Dear has been making things from paper, fabric, and clay for as long as she can remember. She has a head full of ideas and is always working on something new. Aimee rediscovered hand embroidery a few years ago and began designing her own patterns. She is the author of *Doodle-Stitching* and *Doodle-Stitching: The Motif Collection*, two books of contemporary embroidery designs.
www.etsy.com/shop/littledear

How did you discover embroidery as a medium?

My grandma taught me to embroider when I was about five; she used to bring samplers for me to work on when she came to visit. I picked it up again years later and started designing my own patterns. It is the perfect way to bring any idea or sketch to life with thread and fabric. I think I like textile work so much because it's so different from the computer design work I do all day, but still a great creative outlet. There is something primitive and relaxing about stitching something by hand and the result is very special and unique, quite different from the mass-produced items we see so much of.

What is the most challenging part of embroidery?

Embroidery is very easy to learn; it's actually hard to really mess something up. If you don't like something, you can just take out your stitches, or add to them to change them into something different and better. The most challenging part for me is choosing the "right" colors, but that's just because I'm color obsessed!

How do your inspirations translate into beautifully stitched pieces?

I am a constant doodler, and my sketchbook is never far away from me. Many of my quick, random doodles turn into embroidery designs. I like the idea that a little drawing done in seconds can result in a detailed piece of artwork that takes hours or days to complete. I usually start with a fairly complete drawing on fabric, but I am very much a "make it up as I go along" type of person, so freestyle hand embroidery is perfect for my projects. I often end up adding to or changing things as I work.

What essential tip would you give to someone who is just starting to embroider?

Hand embroidery is an easy craft for anyone to pick up. Start by learning one or two basic stitches, and just have fun! You can decide whether to simply follow the pattern lines, or fill in spaces with color or a fun textured stitch, or add details as the ideas come to you.

There are no charts or diagrams and no set rules; it can be as simple as a line drawing or embellishment, or very complex and detailed with lots of different stitches and textures.

As an independent artist, how do you keep your work in the public eye?

I've always posted my work online; that's how my publisher, Lark Books, found me and offered me the chance to write my own books. I continue to keep a crafty blog and a Flickr account, where I post photos of my new projects and patterns. I think sharing your work with other creative people is the best way to advertise, be inspired, and grow as an artist.

Far left: Forest.
Top left: Thinking.
Above: Rainbow Warrior.

Above: Embroidered top from Monsoon.

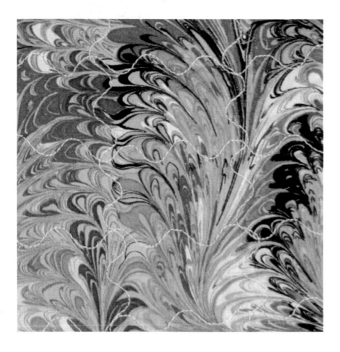

Above: Marbled tote bag by Jan Lorain.

Above: Marbled dress by RE*logyyy.

Above: Laser-cut jacket and skirt by Christopher Kane.

Above: Embroidered dress by Prada.

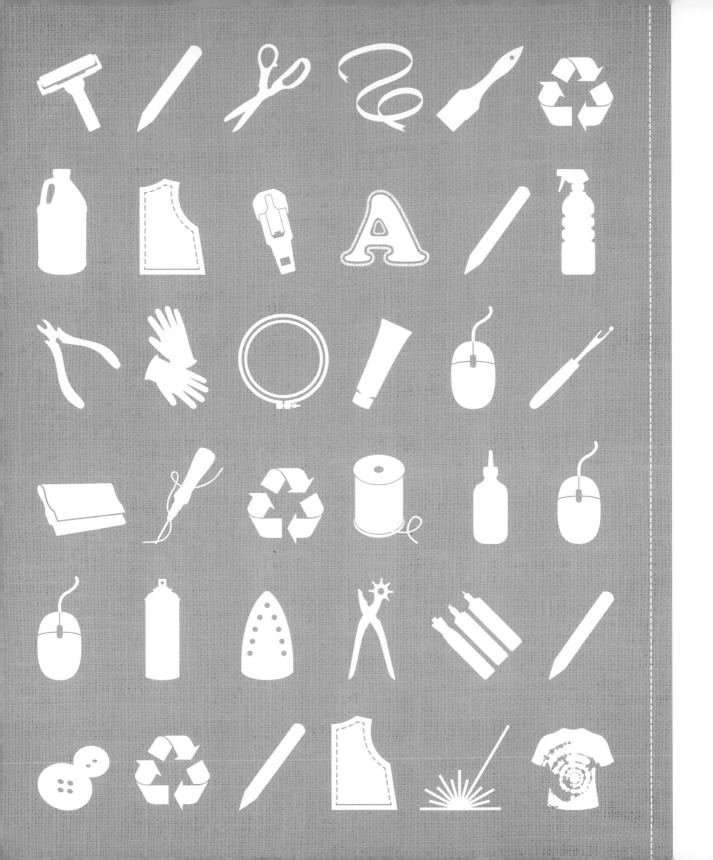

RESOURCES

SUPPLIERS

Beadworks
One of Europe's largest bead suppliers. The range includes gemstones, semiprecious beads, findings, chains, tools, and kits.
www.beadworks.co.uk

Bedecked
Haberdashery and trimmings.
www.bedecked.co.uk

Cloud 9 Fabrics
Eco-friendly, organic fabrics in contemporary designs.
www.cloud9fabrics.com

Cotton Patch
Stocks fabrics, notions, haberdashery, and books.
www.cottonpatch.co.uk

Daisy Janie
Organic cotton fabrics.
www.daisyjanie.com

Dharma Trading Company
Dye and bleaching materials, ready-to-dye blank garments.
www.dharmatrading.com

DMC
International supplier of embroidery threads, fabrics, and accessories.
www.dmc.com

Fabric.com
Discount fabrics and notions, such as zippers, ribbons, and buttons.
www.fabric.com

Fabrics Plus
Fabrics, yarns, accessories, notions, and patterns.
www.fabricsplus.co.uk

Fabric Rehab
Unusual and contemporary fabric designs.
www.fabricrehab.co.uk

Hobby Lobby
Craft supplies, including fabric, beads, sequins, ribbons, and more.
www.hobbylobby.com

John Lewis
British department store with haberdashery department selling fabrics and sewing supplies.
www.johnlewis.com

Liberty
London department store selling fabrics and craft supplies.
www.liberty.co.uk

Loop
Knitting store that also sells unusual haberdashery.
www.loopknittingshop.com

The Makery Emporium
Sells fabric, trimmings, tools, notions, and patterns. Sewing and fashion workshops are held in the store.
www.themakeryonline.com

Michaels
Craft supplies including jewelry findings, paint, dye, soy wax, leather punch, and yarn.
www.michaels.com

M&J Trimming
Suppliers of high-quality trimmings.
www.mjtrim.com

Pro Chemical & Dye
Dye and bleaching materials, printable fabrics, and silks.
www.prochemical.com

Sewing World
Specialist sewing-machine retailer.
www.sewingworld.co.uk

Sharpie
Permanent markers. Totally 80s collection used in Pen and Ink tutorial on page 76.
www.sharpieuncapped.com

Speedball
Rubber pad and carving tools used in Block Print tutorial on page 58, print ink and squeegee used in Screen Print tutorial on page 70.
www.speedballart.com

Spoonflower
Design and print your own fabric or order unique fabrics created by others.
www.spoonflower.com

Threadless
Online community-centered clothing shop. Users submit their T-shirt designs, which are put to a public vote. Winning designs are printed and sold through the shop.
threadless.com

Tim Holtz: Idea-ology Collection
Steampunk Gear Findings used in Toys & Trinkets Tutorial on page 110.
www.timholtz.com/idea-ology.htm

VV Rouleaux
Ribbons and trimmings.
www.vvrouleaux.com

SEWING AND FASHION BLOGS

Bari J.
Online journal of Bari Ackerman, a fabric, sewing pattern, and surface designer.
www.barij.typepad.com

Chictopia
Online fashion community featuring fashion trends, style tips, and a marketplace.
www.chictopia.com

CRAFT Zine
Blog and online magazine dedicated to the renaissance in traditional crafts made in interesting new ways. The blog includes project tutorials and news about a range of crafts.
www.blog.craftzine.com

Crafty Crafty
Projects and ideas for creating and customizing clothes.
www.craftycrafty.tv/custom_clothes

Dear Lizzy
Sewing and craft blog.
www.elizabethkartchner.blogspot.com

DIY Fashion
Blog of fashion and sewing ideas and projects.
www.diyfashion.about.com

DIY Tipps
Step-by-step tutorials for customizing clothes.
www.diy-tipps.onblog.at/en

Elsie Marley
Features craft and sewing tutorials.
www.elsiemarley.com

Face Hunter
Photos of street fashion.
www.facehunter.blogspot.com

Feeling Stitchy
Embroidery blog.
www.feelingstitchy.com

Gemelli
Inspirational handmade projects and tutorials.
www.gemellihandmade.blogspot.com

Green Cotton
Eco-fashion blog featuring trends and issues, as well as highlighting the work of fair trade and ethical designers and companies.
www.greencottonblog.com

Grosgrain
Sewing blog including inspirational images and tutorials.
www.grosgrainfabulous.blogspot.com

Just Chic
Sewing and customizing projects.
www.just-chic.blogspot.com

MADE
Sewing blog with tutorials and patterns.
www.dana-made-it.com

Martha Stewart Crafts
Craft projects, tutorials, and inspirations.
www.thecraftsdept.marthastewart.com

Outsapop
"Trashion" blog of recycled fashion. Includes tutorials, DIY ideas, and styling tips.
www.outsapop.com

The Purl Bee
Fun and approachable sewing, knitting, and crochet projects.
www.purlbee.com

The Sartorialist

Street fashion photo blog.

www.thesartorialist.com

Sew, Mama, Sew!

Fabulous fabric and sewing patterns.

www.sewmamasew.com

The Sewing Divas

Sewing and fashion blog, includes couture techniques and inspirational images.

www.thesewingdivas.wordpress.com

Studs and Pearls

Blog of customizing tutorials.

www.studs-and-pearls.com

Topstylista

Features the latest news from the fashion world.

www.topstylista.com

Virginie Peny

Fashion blog with projects ideas for customizing and reusing clothes.

www.virginiepeny.com

Whip up

Craft blog that brings together a community of artists, crafters, and makers.

www.whipup.net

Wit + Delight

Fashion and design blog written by graphic designer, Kate Gabriel.

www.katearends.com

MAGAZINES

CraftStylish
Tutorials, news, and tips for sewing, knitting, crochet, and more.
www.craftstylish.com

Elle
International fashion magazine.
www.elle.com

Fashionista
Online fashion magazine.
www.fashionista.com

Frankie
Bi-monthly Australian magazine with all the latest news and trends in fashion, craft, art, and more.
www.frankie.com.au

Grazia
Weekly fashion magazine.
www.graziadaily.co.uk

Modern Seamster
Smart, fresh, and innovative sewing magazine.
www.modernseamster.com

Mollie Makes
Lifestyle and craft magazine featuring step-by-step sewing and craft projects.
www.molliemakes.com

Selvedge
Bi-monthly magazine for textile and fashion designers.
www.selvedge.org

Sew Hip
The UK's number one sewing magazine.
www.sewhip.co.uk

Threads Magazine
Magazine for sewing enthusiasts featuring news, projects, and sewing tips.
www.threadsmagazine.com

Trendland
Online fashion, design, and photography magazine.
www.trendland.net

Trashion
Celebrates recycling, creativity, and originality in fashion. Features vintage, customized, handmade, and quirky fashions.
www.trashionmag.com

Vogue
International fashion magazine.
www.vogue.com

BOOKS

200 Projects to Get You Into Fashion Design.
Adrian Grandon and Tracey Fitzgerald.
A&C Black, 2009.

300% Cotton: More T-Shirt Graphics.
Helen Walters.
Laurence King, 2006.

1000 Garment Graphics: A Comprehensive Collection of Wearable Designs.
Jeffrey Evertt.
Rockport, 2009.

Art & Sole: Contemporary Sneaker Design.
Intercity.
Laurence King, 2008.

Cradle to Cradle: Re-making the Way We Make Things.
Michael Braungart and William McDonough.
Vintage, 2009.

Custom Kicks: Personalized Footwear.
Kim Smits and Matthijs Maat.
Laurence King, 2008.

Digital Textile Design.
Melanie Bowles and Ceri Isaac.
Laurence King, 2009.

DIY Fashion: Customize and Personalize.
Selena Francis-Bryden.
Laurence King, 2010.

Doodle Stitching.
Aimee Ray.
Lark Books, 2007.

Doodle Stitching: The Motif Collection.
Aimee Ray.
Lark Books, 2010.

Form, Fit, Fashion: All the Details Fashion Designers Need to Know But Can Never Find.
Jay Calderin.
Rockport, 2009.

Iron Me On: 20 Sheets of Awesome Iron-on Decals.
Mike Perry.
Chronicle Books, 2010.

Junky Styling: Wardrobe Surgery.
Annika Sanders and Kerry Seager.
A&C Black, 2009.

Martha Stewart's Encyclopedia of Sewing and Fabric Crafts.
Martha Stewart.
Potter Craft, 2010.

Mastering the Art of Fabric Printing and Design.
Laurie Wisbrun.
Chronicle Books, 2012.

Sukie Iron-on Craft Pad.
Darrell Gibbs and Julia Harding.
Chronicle Books, 2010.

T-Shirt Factory.
Beams T. Collins
Design, 2007.

Yeah! I Made it Myself: DIY Fashion For The Not Very Domestic Goddess.
Eithne Farry.
W&N, 2006.

SELLING ONLINE

If you want to take it further by selling your creations, or simply want to share your work and ideas, it's never been simpler to get online. You can build an online presence through social networking sites, such as Twitter and Facebook, and share photos of your pieces on sites like Flickr and Pinterest. Sites such as Blogger offer simple ways to set up your own blog.

Artfire
Handmade marketplace and craft community.
www.artfire.com

Etsy
Online marketplace for handmade and vintage items with thousands of sellers from around the world. Etsy is also a good source for unique fabrics, notions, and trimmings.
www.etsy.com

Folksy
Marketplace for buying and selling crafts. Also includes craft tutorials.
www.folksy.com

Zibbet
Marketplace for handmade, vintage, and fine art, plus craft supplies.
www.zibbet.com

GLOSSARY

Acid dye
A dye procedure that uses acidic chemicals, such as vinegar or citric acid, to lower the pH of fibers before dyeing. Acid dye is most effective on protein-based (animal) fibers, such as wool, mohair, alpaca, and silk. It can be used to dye nylon, but is not effective on other synthetic fibers.

Acrylic paint
A water-based paint that is resistant to wash and wear.

Alum
Potassium aluminum sulfate compound used as a mordant in dyeing.

Appliqué
A small piece of fabric that is attached to a larger piece of fabric. It is similar to a patch, but is used primarily for decoration.

Awl
A tool with a long, pointed spike at the end. An awl is useful for pattern marking, as well as for punching holes in leather and thick fabrics.

Backing
Fusible webbing, fabric, or interfacing applied to the back of fabric to give it extra support and shape.

Backstitch
A stitch that runs opposite to the sewing direction. Backstitches are sturdy stitches that can be used to strengthen seams or outline shapes in embroidery.

Batik
A traditional Indonesian dye process that uses wax as a resist. This technique allows a high level of control over where the dye is applied, which means that intricate patterns can be created.

Blanket stitch
A stitch often used to border raw edges to both decorate and reinforce the edge.

Bleaching
The use of chlorine bleach on fabric to remove color. Plant-derived fibers, such as cotton and linen, work best for bleaching projects. Synthetic fabrics, however, such as nylon, acrylic, and polyester, can be severely damaged by bleach.

Bobbin
A cylinder found in the bottom of a sewing machine that holds wound thread. Follow your machine's instructions for winding the bobbin.

Buttonhole stitch
Similar to blanket stitch, this stitch is used to cover and reinforce the raw edges of a buttonhole.

Carbon paper
Paper that has a pigment coating on one side. When pressure is applied, the pigment is transferred onto paper or fabric. Carbon paper is useful for duplicating images.

Carrageenan
A seaweed extract that is used as a thickening and stabilizing agent. In marbling, carrageenan is traditionally used to create a size.

Cellulose fibers
Fibers derived from plants. Cellulose fibers include cotton, rayon, bamboo, hemp, jute, and linen. They generally fare well with a high pH dye process.

Chain stitch
A decorative embroidery stitch often used for outlines and fills.

Collage
A composition made up of many different components, put together to create a single work.

Darning
A series of interwoven running stitches. Darning can be made for decorative or utilitarian purposes; it is especially useful for fixing holes in fabric, most commonly in socks.

Darning egg
A smooth egg-shaped piece of wood used to support the inside of a sock while darning holes.

Darning needle
A large needle with a wide eye that is used for sewing yarn or embroidery thread in long running stitches.

Digital print
An image directly applied to fabric from a printer.

Discharging
The removal of color.

Discharge paste
A paste used for removing color from fabrics. It is commonly used on fabrics that are sensitive to bleach and is most effective on plant-based fibers.

Distressing
The act of purposefully wearing down clothing to make it look old and damaged.

Embellish
To add interest to a piece of clothing by adding elements.

Embroidery
Decorative stitching, most commonly applied to fabric. Embroidery encompasses many different stitches and thread materials.

Embroidery hoop
A frame used to pull fabric taut while stitching.

Embroidery thread
Most commonly, a glossy six-strand floss, spun for embroidery. The strands can be separated to accommodate various kinds of stitching.

Fabric glue
A type of glue designed specifically to hold two pieces of fabric together. Fabric glue can be temporary to aid in sewing, or permanent and able to withstand wash and wear.

Findings
Small auxiliary pieces used in jewelry making. Findings include ear wires, jump-rings, and clasps.

Felt
A matted cloth of woolen fibers.

Foot
See Presser foot

Freezer paper
Paper with a thin plastic coating on one side. It is useful for temporarily adhering and stabilizing fabrics.

French knot
An embroidery stitch that produces a small, twisted knot.

Green fashion
A term used to describe clothing and accessories that are manufactured in environmentally friendly ways and composed of sustainable materials.

Heat setting
The application of heat, such as an iron, to set dyes, inks, and paints on fabric.

Heat transfer paper
Printable paper that can transfer an image to fabric with the application of heat.

Hem
A folded fabric edge that produces a finished look and can prevent unraveling.

Interfacing

An iron-on or sewn-in layer of fabric that provides support and body to the garment. For the projects in this book, we are using fusible, or iron-on, interfacing.

Jump-ring

A circular piece of wire that can be used to attach jewelry components.

Lazy daisy

An embroidery stitch that produces a flower-shaped decoration.

Leather punch

A sturdy metal hole punch specifically designed for easily punching holes in leather.

Marbling fabric

An aqueous surface design technique that produces swirling patterns on fabric.

Marbling size

See Size.

Mordant

A mordant used in dying, such as alum, which creates a bond between the dye and the fabric. Dyes that would not otherwise bond well with the fiber can bond with the mordant instead.

Needle punch

See Punch needle

pH

The measure of acidity of a substance. A low pH is acidic, while a high pH is alkaline (or basic). In dyeing, a high pH is ideal for cellulose fibers, while a low pH is recommended for protein fibers.

Protein fiber

Animal-derived fibers such as wool, angora, mohair, feathers, and cashmere. Animal fibers require a low pH dye process using acid dyes.

Presser foot

An interchangeable sewing machine attachment that holds the fabric in place as you sew and accommodates the type of stitching being done.

Protective gloves

Gloves are required for handling caustic chemicals such as bleach or dye. Rubber and disposable latex gloves work well to prevent irritation.

Punch needle

A hollow needle used to create a looping decorative stitch.

Rotary leather punch

See Leather punch.

Running stitch

A series of stitches quickly made by weaving a threaded needle in and out of fabric.

Satin stitch

A decorative stitch commonly used to fill space in embroidery designs.

Scissors

One of the most often used tools in customizing clothing. Scissors chosen for sewing should only be used on fabric to prevent dulling of the blade.

Screen printing

Printing process where ink is pushed through selected areas of a mesh fabric.

Seam

Where two pieces of fabric are sewn together.

Seam allowance

The width of the raw edges on the inside of a seam.

Seam ripper

A metal tool with a hooked blade, specifically designed to pick out thread without damaging fabric.

Sequins
Decorative disc-shaped beads that are most often shiny and metallic.

Size
In marbling, size is a term used to describe the gelatinous substance that supports the paint. In this book, we use Marbo Gum, a brand of size that is inexpensive and easy to prepare.

Soda ash
Sodium bicarbonate, used to raise the pH of cellulose (plant) fiber before dyeing.

Split stitch
A decorative stitch similar to chain stitch, used to create lines and fills.

Steampunk
The concept of an alternate universe that combines the styles, common building materials, and culture of the steam-powered Victorian and Edwardian eras with those of modern technology.

Stem stitch
A decorative stitch most commonly used to create straight lines, i.e., stems of plants.

Straight pin
A sharp pin used to temporarily hold two pieces of fabric together.

Straight-stitch
A basic in-and-out stitch used to create decorative lines or to bond pieces of fabric together.

Studs
Pronged metal objects used to decorate fabrics.

Synthetic fiber
Man-made fiber such as polyester, spandex, acrylic, and nylon. These fibers can be difficult or even impossible to dye.

Tailor's chalk
When working with fabrics, tailor's chalk is ideal for making temporary marks because it is easily brushed or washed away. It is available in a variety of colors.

Threader
A thin piece of V-shaped wire that is used to guide thread through the eye of a needle.

Tie-dye
A dye process that uses ties or knots in the fabric as a resist.

Upcycle
The act of turning useless or unwanted articles into something of value.

Vinegar
In dyeing fabrics, vinegar is used to lower the pH of protein (animal) fibers to make them more receptive to dyes.

INDEX

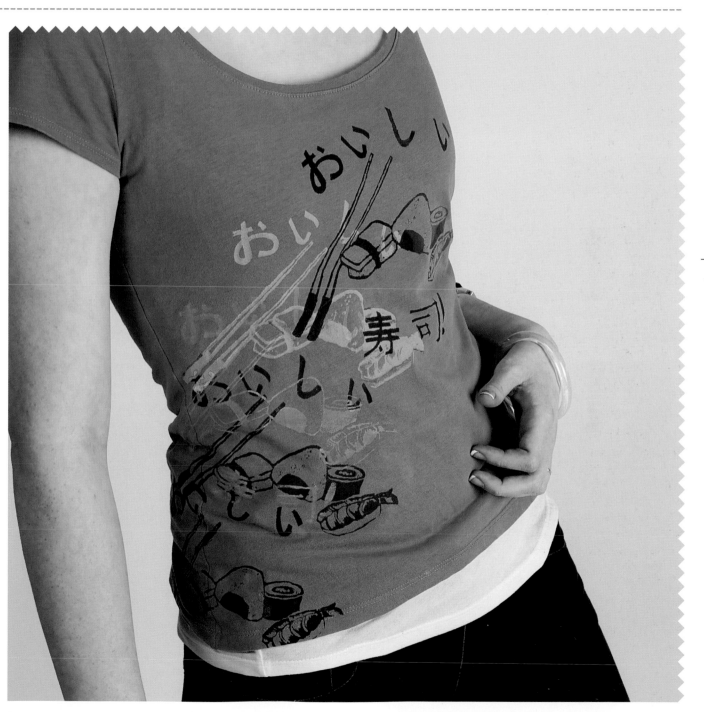

CONTRIBUTORS

Accessorize
www.accessorize.com

Aimee Ray, Little Dear
www.etsy.com/shop/littledear

alice + olivia
www.aliceandolivia.com

Angee W
www.angeew.com

ASOS
www.asos.com

Antik Batik
www.antikbatik.fr

Balmain
www.balmain.com

Beyond Retro
www.beyondretro.com

Bobsmade
www.bobsmade.com

Chris Benz
www.chris-benz.com

Contre le jour
www.etsy.com/shop/ContreLeJour

Daniella Trigo, Screendream
www.etsy.com/shop/screendream

French Connection
www.frenchconnection.com

Gucci
www.gucci.com

Internacionale
www.internacionale.co.uk

Jan Lorain
www.etsy.com/shop/
janandpaulcreations

Jana Foehrenbach, Broken Ghost
Couture
brokenghost.com

Jane Porter
www.etsy.com/shop/janetexcat

Jose Villar
www.joevleather.com

Junky Styling
www.junkystyling.co.uk

Kate Gallagher
www.etsy.com/shop/KatieGallagher

Katie Pray
www.katiepray.com

Lela Rose
www.lelarose.com

Lipsy
www.lipsy.co.uk

Mary Katrantzou
www.marykatrantzou.com

Monsoon
www.monsoon.co.uk

Patricia Valery
patriciavalery.com

People Tree
www.peopletree.co.uk

PopLove Designs
www.etsy.com/shop/poplovedesigns

Prada
www.prada.com

Raygun Robyn
www.raygunrobyn.com

RE*logyyy
www.etsy.com/shop/Relogyyy

River Island
www.riverisland.com

Saija Salminitty, Shadow Empress
Studios
shadowempress.etsy.com

Victoria Dresdner, Batikwalla
www.batikwalla.com

Zero + Maria Cornejo
zeromariacornejo.com

IMAGE CREDITS

ACKNOWLEDGMENTS

Many thanks: To my family and friends, who knew when to ask me how it was going, and when to just ask about the weather. Mr. Todd, who fueled me with peanut butter and mashed potatoes whenever I felt crunchy on the inside; Kurdt, who always lets me call him Jimmy; Evie, who never lets me get away with anything; and Tobey, who asks "any help?"

My sisters, for pushing all my parts back together, even when they didn't know they were doing it; Mom, for crafting me a nice set of brains; Dad, for the need to write and crack wise; and Tim and Tiki, for their huge hearts. Thanks also to Heather, for being the creative matchmaker; Nikki, for all the late night craft-a-thons; Adam for mad robot skills; and Conan O'Brien, for telling me that if you work really hard, and you're kind, amazing things will happen.